TORTURED
FOR
CHRIST

50TH ANNIVERSARY EDITION

TORTURED
FOR
CHRIST

RICHARD WURMBRAND
FOREWORD BY GEORGE VERWER AND DALE RHOTON

David C Cook®
transforming lives together

TORTURED FOR CHRIST:
THE 50TH ANNIVERSARY EDITION
Published by David C Cook
4050 Lee Vance Drive
Colorado Springs, CO 80918 U.S.A.

David C Cook U.K., Kingsway Communications
Eastbourne, East Sussex BN23 6NT, England

The graphic circle C logo is a registered trademark of David C Cook.

At David C Cook, we equip the local church around the
corner and around the globe to make disciples. Come see how
we are working together—go to www.davidccook.com.

The website addresses recommended throughout this book are
offered as a resource to you. These websites are not intended
in any way to be or imply an endorsement on the part of
David C Cook, nor do we vouch for their content.

Unless otherwise noted, Scripture references are taken from the New
King James Version®. Copyright © 1982 by Thomas Nelson. Used by
permission. All rights reserved. Scripture references marked KJV are
taken from the King James Version of the Bible. (Public Domain.)

LCCN 2017946097
ISBN 978-0-8307-7260-5
eISBN 978-0-8307-7262-9

© 1967, 1998, 2013, 2017 The Voice of the Martyrs, Inc.
Previously published by the Living Sacrifice Book Company in 1967
© The Voice of the Martyrs, Inc., ISBN 978-0-88264-057-0.

Cover Design: Amy Konyndyk
Photo Credit: Getty Images

Printed in the United States of America

1 2 3 4 5 6 7 8 9 10

062917

To the Rev. W. Stuart Harris,
General Director of the European Christian
Mission in London, who, upon my release from
prison in 1964, came to Romania as a messenger
from Christians in the West. Entering our house
very late at night, after having taken many
precautionary measures, he brought us words of
love and comfort as well as relief for families of
Christian martyrs. On behalf of these faithful
believers, I hereby express our gratitude.

Contents

Foreword

We saw the Lord open the door for our ministry, Operation Mobilization (OM), to do a significant work in the Communist countries of Eastern Europe and the Soviet Union in the 1960s. We began this work by smuggling literature into these Iron Curtain countries, using secret compartments in our vehicles to take a couple thousand Bibles at a time. We didn't fear being caught by the authorities. But we did ask believers there this question a number of times: "Is it right for us to put your life in jeopardy?" Do you know the answer they always gave? "It is not fair of you to rob us of the opportunity to suffer for our Lord." They were ready. They knew the consequences. They had friends who had been in prison and they were ready to really go for it.

It was exciting to be able to serve these dear people who were suffering so much. It wasn't just one or two believers who went to prison for the Lord. There were many who were faithful to Jesus Christ and ready to face the consequences. I (Dale) remember being at a pastors' lunch in Warsaw, Poland, in the early 1960s. I asked the pastor on my left, "Have you ever been in prison?" He said, "Yes." Then I asked the pastor on my right, "Have you ever been in prison?" He said, "Yes." Then the pastor seated opposite me reached over, grabbed my hands, looked me in the eye, and said, "Don't ask. We have all been in prison." That is a little snapshot of what it was like at the time.

In 1964, we had another experience. We were with three other young men who were also with OM. At the time I was twenty-six years old and the others were a little younger. George and I heard that a Romanian Lutheran pastor had been released after fourteen years in prison in Bucharest. We thought about how nice it would be to visit him. We asked some believers if we could see this man by the name of Richard Wurmbrand. Their initial reaction was negative. "Receiving visitors from the West could complicate things," they said. "Maybe he doesn't want that." We replied, "Could you ask anyway? We would like to meet him but respect if it would complicate his situation." In the end, they said that it would work out.

The five of us with OM walked into a large living room, where five to ten people were seated in a circle. This man who had been in prison for fourteen years was supposed to be among them. I looked around at the group, but no one looked to me like they had been in prison that long. I turned to a young man on my left and asked, "Who has been in prison fourteen years?" He replied, "That man over there." I saw a man whose face was beaming. "How do you know?" I asked this young man. He said, "That is my father."

Now what did Pastor Wurmbrand share that night? What was on his heart after so many years in prison? Here he was, just out of prison, and he talked about wanting to go to the Paris nightclubs and preach the gospel. One of our OM team members present in this meeting had worked in Israel, and Pastor Wurmbrand asked him, "Is there someone in Israel who will help me with what I want to do?" He replied, "There are a number of real fine believers in Israel." The pastor said, "No, don't answer me until I tell you what I want to do." Then he told the man that he wanted to go to the Knesset and preach the gospel. Our team member said, "You know, they will put you in prison for that." Without missing a beat, Pastor Wurmbrand replied, "Yes, I'll get two years." We thought, *Here is a man who was just released from prison and what is he doing? Thinking about how he can get back in prison!* He was a totally different breed.

We visited the Wurmbrands several times while they were in Romania, but my (Dale's) favorite Wurmbrand story is this one. During one visit, I was with them in their home as they were talking in Romanian. I do not understand one word of Romanian, but I could tell they were talking about a person. "Who is this person you are talking about?" I asked. "That is the man who betrayed Richard, and because of him Richard was put in prison," replied his wife, Sabina. Some hours later Richard said, "Dale, let's take a walk." As we were walking, a man crossed the street and came over to us. In Romanian style, Pastor Wurmbrand and this man hugged and kissed, and then he introduced us. The man left, and Richard and I resumed our walk. "That is interesting," I said to Pastor Wurmbrand. "That man has the same name as the man who betrayed you." Without blinking an eye he said, "Dale, we all make mistakes." That was how he was able to dismiss that man's betrayal. I thought that if anybody had injured me at all, I needed only to compare that with what Richard went through and I should be able to forgive pretty easily.

In order to forgive like this, Pastor Wurmbrand must have been totally convinced of the sovereignty of God, that God would somehow take this trial and make something good and powerful out of it. God is able to triumph in all circumstances, and you see it in real life through Christians like Richard Wurmbrand.

What inspired us the most about the way Pastor Wurmbrand lived was his total commitment to Jesus Christ, to know He is truly "the way, the truth, and the life." He could have avoided prison altogether. And once he was in prison, he could have certainly gotten his sentence shortened, but there was no "if" in his life. He was like an arrow shot from a bow that reaches the target no matter what.

Sabina's faith and commitment also inspired us. After the Wurmbrands left Romania, they visited me (Dale) and my wife in Austria. I remember we had devotions together, and Mrs. Wurmbrand stated that Christians have unity. I mentioned to her, "Yes, we should have unity, but sometimes we are not united the way we should be." She cut me off right there and said, "That is true, but Christian unity is different from any other unity. We are not perfect. We make mistakes. We hurt one another. But still, despite all of that, there is something special about Christian unity." She is absolutely right, and I have never forgotten her words.

One time Mrs. Wurmbrand had a request for us: "You smuggle things into the country. Can you smuggle my Bible out of the country?" They had left Romania for the free world, but her Bible was still in Romania. We asked one of our Swedish OM team members to smuggle it out, and she did. When this team member gave it to me, I asked how she smuggled it out of the country. She said, "I put the Bible in this plastic bag and got on the train. I looked at the plastic bag and saw the label 'Old Smuggler Whiskey.'" I said, "At least you were being open about this."

Pastor Wurmbrand didn't dwell on his time in prison. He was a man who was always looking forward: "What can we accomplish? What can we do for others?" These topics came up as we talked with one another. He didn't want to just sit down and say, "Look, here are all the things that I suffered." But he had obviously suffered; he showed us his scars. He heard people in the West were saying, "Communism isn't so bad. That is just another philosophy and economics." He said, "The West has been deluded and they have to understand what communism really is." One of the first countries Richard visited when he left Romania was Italy, where he met a man who told him, "I am a Baptist and a Communist." Richard told him, "That can't be."

We knew the message in this book was so important. It's a message that was important not only in Italy or the United States, but all around the world. In a letter to Pastor Wurmbrand from me (George) in 1968, I told him:

> First of all, let me tell you that God is really using your book *Tortured for Christ* in a tremendous way here in India....
>
> We have also been able to publicly tell a little bit about your testimony, and God has used this

as a knife to cut into the hearts of many sleeping Christians. Recently, up in the hills where I was ministering to missionaries and Christian workers from all over India, I was able to tell a little bit of your story, and I had only wished that I had copies of your book with me at the time.

There is a blindness and an apathy toward communism here in India that is almost beyond description. As you know, the Communists are moving in a tremendous way and have already taken over the State of Kerala. They have of course made many other gains in a few other states, and it is almost impossible to go through the streets of any city without seeing the Reds on the march.

The Christian church is almost totally ignorant of the real ways of communism here and perhaps as you know, the Indian church is known for its ecumenical spirit. They have no idea that Christians are suffering behind the Iron Curtain.

I could literally give a page full of reasons concerning why I believe your books and other Christ-centered, God-exalting literature must be flooded out across this nation.

We are thankful for Richard and Sabina. We thank God for every one of our brothers and sisters ministering to people who are being persecuted. The Lord knows there are people right now who are walking in the shoes of Richard and Sabina Wurmbrand, and we pray for God's grace and protection and blessing. May they see the hand of God!

May this book open the eyes of all who read it to God's great purposes around the world!

—George Verwer and Dale Rhoton,
founders of Operation Mobilization

Introduction

Richard Wurmbrand

The Man and His Message

I first read *Tortured for Christ* in 1968, not long after it was published, and then several friends quickly issued an invitation to Richard Wurmbrand to visit Australia. We knew nothing about the man apart from what we had read in his book, but sensed that he was a man sent from God with a burning heart and an urgent message. His message was needed as a clarion call to the slumbering, and oft-times indifferent, church in the Western free world. That call I dare to say is still needed today—a call for Christians who live in an atmosphere of freedom and plenty to seriously heed the words in the book of Hebrews to remember God's children in the difficult places of this world where they are fiercely persecuted and imprisoned, because they bravely proclaim the name of the Lord Jesus Christ.

On August 1, 1969, Reg Werry, another friend, and I welcomed Richard Wurmbrand to Australia at the Sydney Airport. At that moment I had no idea that Pastor Wurmbrand's message would burn its way into my own heart and begin a friendship and working relationship that would last until Richard's call home in 2001.

The conditions and atmosphere that Richard left behind in Romania were never far from him. Through secret channels he continued to be in touch with the Underground Church behind the Iron Curtain. I saw him weep often as he received news and relived the heartache and suffering of being under the heel of atheistic communism. I well remember walking into his hotel room one day to find him pacing the room, wringing his hands in a spirit of agitation and agony of heart. He had just heard on television about a major disturbance in Israel and of the injuries and deaths of those involved. I mistakenly assumed they were friends or acquaintances, but no—his empathy was such that his heart bled for the victims of any kind of torture or harassment. I heard him take the defense of Communists who were tortured, saying that not even murderers should suffer torture. He desired to repay the Communists for the terrible deeds they had perpetrated by showing them the beauty of Christ and winning their hearts for Him.

Pastor Wurmbrand loved the gospel and was a gifted evangelist. He was well known in Romania for his dedication to the gospel ministry. Even in his prison circumstances he looked for opportunities to tell people about Christ. We know he won not only fellow prisoners but also some of his jailers to the Lord. I remember having the privilege of visiting our mission in Germany—West Germany as it was then known. Richard Wurmbrand was one of the speakers for an event they had organized. Before the meeting began, I was standing in the parking lot, talking with Richard when a car came down the road and stopped to let somebody out. Richard touched my arm to excuse himself and went immediately to warmly embrace the new arrival. I heard them speaking in Romanian and concluded they were coworkers from the Underground Church in Bucharest. I inquired later to discover the friend he greeted so warmly had been one of his jailers and torturers in Romania who had come to the Lord through Richard's witness in prison. It was a decision that would cost the man time in prison because he tried to help some of the Christian prisoners.

On Richard's first day in Australia, we took him to a hotel in Sydney and told him he was free until the following day. He'd flown in from a busy month of meetings in New Zealand, so we left him at the hotel to rest and be refreshed, for another month of preaching engagements would start the next evening. When we came for him the following day, he told us that the previous evening he had gone for a walk, and after a short distance found himself in Sydney's infamous "red light" district of Kings Cross. He noticed a brightly decorated establishment that seemed to be some kind of nightclub and decided to go in. The six-foot-three pastor was dressed in a dark suit and wore a clerical collar. He walked into the dimly lit, smoke-filled establishment and paused as a quiet hush descended. Remember this was 1969. People were sitting at tables with their drinks and cigarettes, watching scantily clad girls cavorting on a dais in the center of the room. Richard boldly stepped forward to stand among the tables, and as people held their breath, he quickly introduced himself and told them God loved them and Christ died for them. Then he left the building and went on his way.

The gospel was very dear to him, but one day Richard said to me something like this: "Nobody knows how much I miss baptizing a baby, marrying a couple, serving Holy Communion, preaching the gospel—all those things that are part of a pastor's heart and his normal activity." He paused, then continued, "God has called me to lay those things aside to use my time and energy to speak for those who are persecuted … and this one thing I do."

I also remember one Sunday in Melbourne, Australia. Richard had preached in the morning. Now we were sitting at the table, enjoying lunch. About eight of us were present, and I was seated opposite Richard. At some point during the meal the doorbell rang and our host went to see who was calling. There was the muffled sound of conversation, and then our host stood in the doorway with a policeman in uniform. As I looked at Richard, who had been telling us a story, he became silent and turned white as the blood drained from his face. After a momentary silence, he recovered his composure and continued his story. Our host was an official of some kind, and the police officer had come to have him sign a document that was urgent. In a few minutes he was gone.

Richard explained his reaction. He told us it was just like that when he lived in Communist Romania. He would be sitting at the table with friends in their house, he said, when the host would open the door for members of the secret police to enter and make arrests. He told us that many times faithful believers were betrayed by their friends or even church leaders. The experiences of the past were still vivid in his memory, and this simple event had been a stunning and disturbing reminder. For us it was a graphic example of the conditions faced by our brothers and sisters in restricted nations. (Editor's note: Soon after Richard left Australia, Merv and Reg founded The Voice of the Martyrs in Australia.)

The message of *Tortured for Christ*, as it tells the agonizing but triumphant story of the persecuted church behind the Iron Curtain, is as urgent today as it was fifty years ago. The violent world in which we live has fostered the growth of many ideological "isms" antagonistic to the gospel of Jesus Christ and His church. We rest our weary hearts in the promise that Christ made when He said, "I will build My church, and the gates of Hades shall not prevail against it" (Matthew 16:18). He assured us, "If they persecuted Me, they will also persecute you" (John 15:20).

Christians who study the Word recognize the times in which we live and look forward to the return of Christ. But in doing so, we understand, and indeed we experience, the turmoil and the terror that will lead to that glorious event. Richard Wurmbrand's message in this book is a gift from God to His children who are called to face the trauma of this age, to stand up and be counted for righteousness' sake against unmitigated evil. This book is an encouragement to "Take up the whole armor of God, that you may be able to withstand in the evil day, and having done all, to stand" (Ephesians 6:13).

Tortured for Christ is a vital message for today.

—*Merv Knight, Wurmbrand historian and cofounder of The Voice of the Martyrs, Australia*

Chapter 1

The Russians' Avid Thirst for Christ

An Atheist Finds Christ

I was orphaned from the first years of life. Being brought up in a family in which no religion was recognized, I received no religious education as a child. As the result of a bitter childhood, which included knowing poverty in the difficult years of World War I, at age fourteen I was as convinced an atheist as the Communists are today. I had read atheistic books, and it was not just that I did not believe in God or Christ—I hated these notions, considering them harmful for the human mind. So I grew up in bitterness toward religion.

But as I understood afterward, I had the grace to be one of the chosen of God for reasons that I don't understand. These reasons had nothing to do with my character, because my character was very bad.

Although I was an atheist, something unreasonable always attracted me to churches. I found it difficult to pass a church without entering it. However, I never understood what was happening in these churches. I listened to the sermons, but they didn't appeal to my heart. I had an image of God as a master whom I should have to obey. I hated this wrong image of God that I had in my mind, but I would have liked very much to know that a loving heart existed somewhere in the center of this universe. Since I had known few of the joys of childhood and youth, I longed that there should be a loving heart beating for me, too.

I convinced myself that there was no God, but I was sad that such a God of love did not exist. Once, in my inner spiritual conflict, I entered a Catholic church. I saw people kneeling and saying something. I thought, *I will kneel near them so I can hear what they say and repeat the prayers to see if something happens.* They said a prayer to the holy virgin, "Hail Mary, full of grace." I repeated the words after them again and again; I looked at the statue of the virgin Mary, but nothing happened. I was very sad about it.

One day, being a very convinced atheist, I prayed to God. My prayer was something like this: "God, I know surely that You do not exist. But if perchance You exist, which I contest, it is not my duty to believe in You; it is Your duty to reveal Yourself to me." I was an atheist, but atheism did not give peace to my heart.

During this time of inner turmoil, an old carpenter in a village high up in the mountains of Romania prayed like this: "My God, I have served you on earth and I wish to have my reward on earth as well as in heaven. And my reward should be that I should not die before I bring a Jew to Christ, because Jesus was from the Jewish people. But I am poor, old, and sick. I cannot go around and seek a Jew. In my village there are none. Bring a Jew into my village and I will do my best to bring him to Christ."

Something irresistible drew me to that village. I had no reason to go there. Romania has twelve thousand villages, but I went to *that* one. Seeing I was a Jew, the carpenter courted me as never a beautiful girl had been courted. He saw in me the answer to his prayer and gave me a Bible to read. I had read the Bible out of cultural interest many times before. But the Bible he gave me was another kind of Bible. As he told me some time later, he and his wife prayed together for hours for my conversion and that of my wife. The Bible he gave me was written not so much in words, but in flames of love fired by his prayers. I could barely read it. I could only weep over it, comparing my bad life with the life of Jesus; my impurity with His righteousness; my hatred with His love—and He accepted me as one of His own.

Soon thereafter, my wife was converted. She brought other souls to Christ. Those other souls brought still more souls to Christ, and so a new Lutheran congregation arose in Romania.

Then came the Nazis under whom we suffered much. In Romania, Nazism took the form of a dictatorship of extreme orthodox elements that persecuted Protestant groups as well as the Jews.

Even before my formal ordination and before I was prepared for the ministry, I was the leader of this church, being the founder of it. I was responsible for it. My wife and I were arrested several times, beaten, and hauled before Nazi judges. The Nazi terror was great, but only a taste of what was to come under the Communists.

My son, Mihai, had to assume a non-Jewish name to prevent his death.

But these Nazi times had one great advantage. They taught us that physical beatings could be endured, and that the human spirit with God's help can survive horrible tortures. They taught us the technique of secret Christian work, which was a preparation for a far worse ordeal to come—an ordeal that was just before us.

My Ministry to the Russians

Out of remorse for having been an atheist, I longed from the first day of my conversion to be able to witness to the Russians. The Russians are a people raised from childhood in atheism. My desire to reach Russians has been fulfilled, and I did not have to go to Russia to reach them. Its fulfillment began in Nazi times, because we had in Romania many thousands of Russian war prisoners among whom we could do Christian work.

It was a dramatic, moving work. I will never forget my first encounter with a Russian prisoner, an engineer. I asked him if he believed in God. If he had said "no," I would not have minded it much. It is the choice of every man to believe or disbelieve. But when I asked him this, he lifted his eyes toward me without understanding and said, "I have no such military order to believe. If I have an order I will believe."

Tears ran down my cheeks. I felt my heart torn in pieces. Here stood before me a man whose mind was dead, a man who had lost a great gift God has given to mankind—his individuality. He was a brainwashed tool in the hands of the Communists, ready to believe or not on an order. He could not think anymore on his own. This was a typical Russian after all these years of Communist domination! After the shock of seeing what communism had done to human beings, I promised God that I would dedicate my life to these men, to give them back their personalities and to give them faith in God and Christ.

Beginning August 23, 1944, one million Russian troops entered Romania and, very soon after this, the Communists came to power in our country. Then began a nightmare that made suffering under the Nazis seem easy.

At that time in Romania, which now has a population of about 24 million, the Communist party had only ten thousand members. But Vishinsky, the Foreign Secretary of the Soviet Union, stormed into the office of our much beloved King Michael I, pounded his fists on the table and said, "You must appoint Communists to the government." Our army and police were disarmed and so, by violence and hated by almost all, the Communists came to power. It was not without the cooperation of the American and British rulers of that time.

Men are responsible before God not only for their personal sins, but also for their national sins. The tragedy of all the captive nations is a responsibility on the hearts of American and British Christians. Americans must know that they have at times unwittingly assisted the Russians in imposing upon us a regime of murder and terror. As a part of the Body of Christ, Americans must atone for this by helping the captive peoples come to the light of Christ.

The Seduction of the Church

Once the Communists came to power, they skillfully used the means of seduction toward the Church. The language of love and the language of seduction are the same. The one who wishes a girl for a wife and the one who wishes her for only a night both say the words, "I love you." Jesus has told us to discern between the language of seduction and the language of love, and to know the wolves clad in sheepskin from the real sheep. Unfortunately, when the Communists came to power, thousands of priests, pastors, and ministers did not know how to discern between the two voices.

The Communists convened a congress of all Christian bodies in our Parliament building. There were four thousand priests, pastors, and ministers of all denominations—and these men of God chose Joseph Stalin as honorary president of this congress. At the same time he was president of the World Movement of the Godless and a mass murderer of Christians. One after another, bishops and pastors arose and declared that communism and Christianity are fundamentally the same and could coexist. One minister after another said words of praise toward communism and assured the new government of the loyalty of the Church.

My wife and I were present at this congress. Sabina told me, "Richard, stand up and wash away this shame from the face of Christ! They are spitting in His face." I said to her, "If I do so, you lose your husband." She replied, "I don't wish to have a coward as a husband."

Then I arose and spoke to this congress, praising not the murderers of Christians, but Jesus Christ, stating that our loyalty is due first to Him. The speeches at this congress were broadcast and the whole country could hear proclaimed from the rostrum of the Communist Parliament the message of Christ! Afterward I had to pay for this, but it was worthwhile.

Orthodox and Protestant church leaders competed with each other in yielding to communism. An Orthodox bishop put the hammer and sickle on his robes and asked his priests to no longer call him "Your Grace," but "Comrade Bishop." Priests like Patrascoiu and Rosianu were more direct. They became officers of the secret police. Rapp, deputy bishop of the Lutheran church in Romania, began to teach in the theological seminary that God had given three revelations: one through Moses, one through Jesus, and the third through Stalin, the last superseding the one before.

I attended the Congress of the Baptists in the town of Resita—a congress under the Red flag, where the anthem of the Soviet Union had been sung with everyone standing. The president of the Baptists praised Stalin as a great teacher of the Bible and proclaimed Stalin did nothing but fulfill the commandments of God!

It must be understood that the true Baptists, whom I love very much, did not agree and were very faithful to Christ, suffering much. However, the Communists "elected" their leaders and the Baptists had no choice but to accept them. The same condition exists today in Communist nations among the very top religious leadership of the "official"[1] church. Those who became servants of communism instead of Christ began to denounce the brethren who did not join them.

Just as Christians in Russia created an Underground Church after their revolution, the coming to power of communism and the betrayal by many official church leaders compelled us to likewise create in Romania an Underground Church: one faithful to evangelize, preach the gospel, and reach children for Christ. The Communists forbade all this and the official church complied.

Together with others, I began an underground work. Outwardly I had a very respectable position—pastor of the Norwegian Lutheran Mission—that served as a cover for my real underground work. At the same time I represented the World Council of Churches in Romania. (In Romania we had not the slightest idea that this organization would ever cooperate with the Communists. At that time in our country it did nothing but relief work.) These two titles gave me a very good standing before the authorities, who did not know of my underground work.

There were two aspects of this underground work. The first was our secret ministry among Russian soldiers. The second aspect was our underground work with the enslaved peoples of Romania.

---

1   The official church is one registered with and controlled by the government. Membership of official churches in many totalitarian systems today is usually less than ten percent of the Christian population. The others prefer to worship "underground."

Russians—A People with Such "Thirsty" Souls

For me, to preach the gospel to the Russians is heaven on earth. I have preached the gospel to men of many nations, but I have never seen a people drink in the gospel like the Russians. They have such thirsty souls.

An Orthodox priest, a friend of mine, telephoned me and told me that a Russian officer had come to him to confess. My friend did not know Russian. However, knowing that I speak Russian, he had given him my address. The next day this man came to see me. He longed for God, but he had never seen a Bible. He had no religious education and never attended religious services (churches in Russia then were very scarce). He loved God without the slightest knowledge of Him.

I read to him the Sermon on the Mount and the parables of Jesus. After hearing them, he danced around the room in rapturous joy proclaiming, "What a wonderful beauty! How could I live without knowing this Christ!" It was the first time that I saw someone so joyful in Christ.

Then I made a mistake. I read to him the passion and crucifixion of Christ, without having prepared him for this. He had not expected it and, when he heard how Christ was beaten, how He was crucified and that in the end He died, he fell into an armchair and began to weep bitterly. He had believed in a Savior and now his Savior was dead!

I looked at him and was ashamed. I had called myself a Christian, a pastor, and a teacher of others, but I had never shared the sufferings of Christ as this Russian officer now shared them. Looking at him, it was like seeing Mary Magdalene weeping at the foot of the cross, faithfully weeping when Jesus was a corpse in the tomb.

Then I read to him the story of the resurrection and watched his expression change. He had not known that his Savior arose from the tomb. When he heard this wonderful news, he beat his knees and swore—using very dirty, but very "holy" profanity. This was his crude manner of speech. Again he rejoiced, shouting for joy, "He is alive! He is alive!" He danced around the room once more, overwhelmed with happiness!

I said to him, "Let us pray!" He did not know how to pray. He did not know our "holy" phrases. He fell on his knees together with me and his words of prayer were: "Oh God, what a fine chap you are! If I were You and You were me, I would never have forgiven You of Your sins. But You are really a very nice chap! I love You with all of my heart."

I think that all the angels in heaven stopped what they were doing to listen to this sublime prayer from a Russian officer. The man had been won for Christ!

In a shop, I met a Russian captain with a lady officer. They were buying all kinds of things and had difficulty speaking to the salesman, who did not understand Russian. I offered to translate for them and we became acquainted. I invited them to lunch at our house. Before beginning to eat, I told them, "You are in a Christian house and we have the habit of praying." I said the prayer in Russian. They put down their forks and knives and were no longer interested in food. Instead, they asked question after question about God, Christ, and the Bible. They knew nothing.

It was not easy to talk to them. I told them the parable of the man who had a hundred sheep and lost one. They did not understand, as they were brainwashed with the Communist ideology. They asked, "How is it that he has a hundred sheep? Has not the Communist collective farm taken them away?" Then I said that Jesus is a king. They answered, "All the kings have been bad men who controlled the people, so Jesus must also be a dictator." When I told them the parable of the workers in the vineyard, they said, "Well, these did very well to rebel against the owner of the vineyard. The vineyard has to belong to the collective." Everything was new for them. When I told them about the birth of Jesus, they asked what would seem blasphemous to a Westerner, "Was Mary the wife of God?" In talking with them and many others, I learned that to preach the gospel to the Russians, after so many years of communism, we had to use an entirely new approach.

This truth applies in many different cultures. The missionaries who went to Central Africa had difficulty translating the words of Isaiah: "Though your sins are like scarlet, they shall be white as snow" (1:18). No one in Central Africa had ever seen snow, so they had no word for it. The missionaries had to translate, "Your sins will become white as the kernel of the coconut."

So we had to translate the gospel into the "Marxist language" in order for them to identify with it. It was something we could not do by ourselves, but the Holy Spirit did His work through us.

The captain and the lady officer were converted on that day. Later, they helped us much in our underground ministry to the Russians.

We secretly printed and distributed among Russians many thousands of Gospels and other Christian literature. Through the converted Russian soldiers, we smuggled Bibles and Bible portions into Russia. We also used another technique to get copies of God's Word into the hands of Russians. The Russian soldiers had been fighting for several years and many of them had children back home whom they had not seen for all this time. (The Russians have a great fondness for children.) My son, Mihai, and other children under ten years of age would go to the Russian soldiers on the streets and in the parks, carrying Bibles, Gospels, and other literature in their pockets. The Russian soldiers would pat them on the head, talk to them lovingly, thinking of their own children whom they had not seen in years. The soldiers would give them chocolate or candy, and the children, in turn, would give the soldiers something—Bibles and Gospels, which they eagerly accepted. Often what was too dangerous for us to do openly our children did in complete safety. They were "young missionaries" to the Russians. The results were excellent. Many Russian soldiers received the gospel this way when there was no other way to give it to them.

Preaching in Russian Army Barracks

We worked among the Russians not only by individual witnessing. We were able to work in small group meetings as well.

The Russians were very fond of watches. They stole watches from everyone. They would stop people on the street and demand that they hand them over. We would see Russians with several watches on each arm, and Russian women officers with alarm clocks hanging around their necks. They had never had watches before and could not get enough of them. Romanians who wished to have a watch had to go to the barracks of the Soviet army to buy a stolen one, often buying back their own watch. So it was common for Romanians to enter the Russian barracks. The Underground Church also used that pretext—of purchasing watches from them—to give us entrance into their barracks.

The first time I preached in a Russian barrack was on the day of St. Paul and St. Peter, an Orthodox feast. I went onto the military base pretending to buy a watch. I pretended that one was too expensive, another was too small, and another too big. Several soldiers crowded around me, each offering me something to buy. Jokingly I asked them, "Are any of you named Paul or Peter?" Some were. Then I said, "Do you know that today is the day when your Orthodox church honors St. Paul and St. Peter?" (Some of the older Russians knew it.) So I asked, "Do you know who Paul and Peter were?" No one knew, so I began to tell them about Paul and Peter. One of the older Russian soldiers interrupted me and said, "You have not come to buy watches. You have come to tell us about the faith. Sit down here with us and speak to us! But be very careful! We know about whom to beware. These around me are all good men, but when I put my hand on your knee, you must talk only about watches. When I remove my hand, you may begin your message again."

Quite a great crowd of men was gathered around me and I told them about Paul and Peter, about the Christ for whom Paul and Peter died. From time to time, someone would approach in whom they had no confidence. The soldier would put his hand on my knee and I would talk about watches. When that man went away, I resumed preaching about Christ. This visit was repeated numerous times with the help of Russian Christian soldiers. Many of their comrades found Christ and thousands of Gospels were given out secretly.

A number of our brothers and sisters in the Underground Church were caught and heavily beaten for this, but they didn't betray our organization.

During this work we had the joy of meeting brethren from the Underground Church in Russia and hearing about their experiences. First of all, we saw in them the makings of great saints. They had passed through so many years of Communist indoctrination. But just as a fish lives in the salty waters and keeps its meat sweet, they passed through the Communist schools and universities but had kept their souls clean and pure in Christ.

These Russian Christians had such beautiful souls! They said, "We know that the star with the hammer and sickle, which we wear on our caps, is the star of the anti-Christ." They said this with great sorrow. They helped us greatly to spread the gospel among other Russian soldiers.

I can say that they had all the Christian virtues, except the virtue of joy. This they had only at conversion, then it disappeared. I thought about this a lot. Once I asked a Baptist, "How is it that you know no joy?" He answered, "How can I be joyful when I have to hide from the pastor of my church that I am an earnest Christian, that I lead a life of prayer, that I try to win souls? The pastor of the church is an informer of the secret police. We are spied on one after another and the shepherds are those who betray the flock. There exists very deep in our heart the joy of salvation, but this external gladness that you have—we do not have it anymore."

Christianity has become dramatic with us. When Christians in free countries win a soul for Christ, the new believer may become a member of a quietly living church. But when those in captive nations win someone, we know that he may have to go to prison and that his children may become orphans. The joy of having brought someone to Christ is always mixed with this feeling that there is a price that must be paid. We had met an entirely new type of Christian—the Christian of the Underground Church.

Here we had many surprises.

As there are many who believe they are Christians and in reality are not, we found that among the Russians there are many who believe they are atheists, but in reality they are not.

On a train, a Russian officer sat in front of me. I had spoken to him about Christ for only a few minutes when he broke out with a torrent of atheistic arguments. Quotations from Marx, Stalin, Voltaire, Darwin, and others against the Bible just flew from his mouth. He gave me no opportunity to contradict him. He spoke for nearly an hour to convince me that there is no God. When he had finished, I asked him, "If there is no God, why do you pray when you are in trouble?" Like a thief surprised while stealing, he replied,

"How do you know that I pray?" I did not allow him to escape. "I asked my question first. I asked why you pray. Please answer!" He bowed his head and acknowledged, "On the front, when we were encircled by the Germans, we all prayed! We did not know how to do it. So we said, 'God and spirit of mother'"—which is surely a very good prayer in the sight of the One who looks to the heart.

I met a Russian couple, both sculptors. When I spoke to them about God, they answered, "No, God does not exist. We are *bezboshniki*—godless. But we will tell you something interesting that happened to us.

"Once we worked on a statue of Stalin. During the work, my wife asked me, 'How about the thumb? If we did not have an opposing thumb—if our fingers were like our toes—we could not hold a hammer, mallet, tool, book, or piece of bread. Human life would be impossible without this little thumb. Now, who made the thumb? We both learned Marxism in school and know that heaven and earth exist by themselves. They are not created by God. So I have learned and so I believe. But if God did not create heaven and earth, if He created only the thumb, He would be praiseworthy for this little thing.

"'We praise Edison and Bell and Stephenson who have invented the electric bulb, telephone, railway, and other things. But why should we not praise the One who has invented the thumb? If Edison had not had a thumb, he would have invented nothing. It is only right to worship God who made the thumb.'"

The husband became very angry, as husbands very often do when their wives tell them wise things. "Don't speak stupidities!

You have learned that there is no God. You do not know if the house is bugged. We can get into trouble. Get into your mind *once and for all* that there is no God. In heaven there is *nobody!*"

She replied, "This is an even greater wonder. If in heaven there is an Almighty God, in whom in stupidity our forefathers believed, it would then be only natural that we should have thumbs. An Almighty God can do everything, so He can make a thumb, too. But if in heaven there is nobody, I will worship with all of my heart the 'Nobody' who has made the thumb."

So they became worshipers of the "Nobody"! Their faith in this "Nobody" increased with time, believing Him to be the creator not only of the thumb, but also of the stars, flowers, children, and everything beautiful in life. It was just as in Athens in earlier times, when Paul met worshipers of the "unknown God" (Acts 17:23).

This couple was unspeakably happy to hear from me that they had believed rightly, that in heaven there is really a "No-body"—God who is Spirit. He is a Spirit of love, wisdom, truth, and power, who so loved them that He sent His only begotten Son to sacrifice Himself for them on the cross.

They had been believers in God not knowing that they were so. I had the great privilege of taking them one step further—to the experience of salvation and redemption.

Once I saw a Russian lady officer on the street. I approached her and apologized, "I know that it is impolite to approach an unknown lady on the street, but I am a pastor and my intentions are earnest. I wish to speak to you about Christ."

She asked me, "Do you love Christ?" I said, "Yes! With all of my heart." She fell into my arms and kissed me again and again. It was a very embarrassing situation for a pastor, so I kissed her back, hoping people would think we were relatives. She exclaimed to me, "I love Christ, too!" I took her to our home and discovered to my amazement that she knew nothing about Christ—absolutely nothing—except the name. And yet she loved Him. She did not know that He is the Savior, nor what salvation means. She did not know where and how He lived and died. She did not know His teachings, His life or ministry. She was for me a psychological curiosity: how can you love someone if you know only his name?

When I inquired, she explained, "As a child, I was taught to read by pictures. For an 'a' there was an apple, for 'b' there was a bell, for 'c' a cat, and so on.

"When I went to high school, I was taught that it was my holy duty to defend the Communist fatherland. I was taught about Communist morals. But I did not know what a 'holy duty' or a 'moral' looked like. I needed a picture for these. Now, I knew that our forefathers had a picture for everything beautiful, praiseworthy, and truthful in life. My grandmother always bowed before this picture, saying that it was the picture of one called *Cristos* (Christ). And I loved this name by itself. This name became so real to me! Just to say this name gave me such joy."

Listening to her, I remembered what is written in Philippians 2:10, that at the name of Jesus every knee should bow. Perhaps the anti-Christ will be able for a time to erase from the world the knowledge of God. But there is power in the simple name of Christ, and this will lead one to the light.

She joyously found Christ in my home and now the One whose name she loved lived in her heart.

Every moment I lived with Russians was full of poetry and deep meaning. A sister who spread the gospel in railway stations gave an interested officer my address. One evening he entered my house—a tall, handsome Russian lieutenant.

I asked him, "How can I serve you?"

He answered, "I have come for light."

I began to read him the most essential parts of Scripture. He put his hand upon mine and said, "I ask you with all of my heart, don't lead me astray. I belong to a people kept in the dark. Tell me, please, is this the true Word of God?" I assured him that it was. He listened for hours—and accepted Christ.

Russians are rarely superficial or shallow in religious matters. Whether they fought against religion or were for it and sought Christ, they put their whole soul into it. That is why under communism in Russia, Christians were soul-winning missionaries. Russians are also historically a religious people. Countries such as this are ripe and fruitful for gospel work, and the course of the world is being changed as we aggressively share the gospel with them. It is such a tragedy that Russia and its peoples are very hungry for the Word of God, yet many have seemingly written them off.

Our ministry to the Russians has borne much fruit.

I remember Piotr (Peter). No one knows in what Russian prison he disappeared. He was so young—perhaps twenty. He had come to Romania with the Russian army. He was converted in an underground meeting and asked me to baptize him.

After his baptism, I asked him to tell us what verse of the Bible had impressed him most and had influenced him to come to Christ.

He said that at one of our secret meetings, I had read Luke 24, the story of Jesus meeting the two disciples who went toward Emmaus. When they drew near the village, "He [Jesus] indicated that He would have gone farther" (verse 28). Piotr said, "I wondered why Jesus said this. He surely wanted to stay with His disciples. Why then did He say that He wished to go further?" My explanation was that Jesus is polite. He wished to be very sure that He was desired. When He saw that He was welcomed, He gladly entered the house with them. The Communists are impolite. They enter by violence into our hearts and minds. They force us to listen to them from morning to late in the night. They do it through their schools, radio, newspapers, posters, movies, atheistic meetings, and everywhere we turn. We have to listen continuously to their godless propaganda whether we like it or not. Jesus respects our freedom. He gently knocks at the door of our heart.

"Jesus has won me by His politeness," said Piotr. This stark contrast between communism and Christ had convinced him. He was not the only Russian to have been impressed by this feature in Jesus' character. (As a pastor, I had never thought about it this way.)

After his conversion, Piotr repeatedly risked his liberty and life to smuggle Christian literature and help for the Underground

Church in Romania to Russia. In the end he was caught. The last I heard of him, he was still in prison. Did he die? Is he already in heaven or is he continuing the good fight on earth? I don't know. Only God knows where he is today.

Like Piotr, many others were not just converted. We should never stop at having won a soul for Christ. By this, we have done only half the work. Every soul won for Christ must be made to be a soul-winner. The Russians were not only converted, but became "missionaries" in the Underground Church. They were reckless and daring for Christ, always saying that it was the least they could do for Christ who died for them.

Our Underground Ministry to an Enslaved Nation

The second aspect of our ministry was our underground missionary work among Romanians.

Initially, the Communists used seduction to win church leaders to their side, but very soon they dropped their masks. Then the terror began and thousands were arrested. To win a soul for Christ began to be a dramatic thing for us, too, as it had long been for the Russians.

For example, I was later in prison together with souls whom God had helped me to win for Christ. I was in the same cell with one who had left behind six children and who was now in prison for his Christian faith. His wife and children were starving. He might never see them again. I asked him, "Have you any resentment against me that I brought you to Christ and because of this your family is in such misery?" He answered, "I have no words to express my thankfulness that you have brought me to the wonderful Savior. I would never have it any other way."

Preaching in these new conditions was not easy. Our people were very oppressed. The Communists took possessions from everyone. From the farmer they took fields and sheep. From a barber or tailor, they took his little shop. It was not only the capitalists who were expropriated; very poor men also suffered much. Nearly every family had a member in prison, and the poverty was great. Men asked, "How is it that a God of love permits the triumph of evil?"

It likewise would not have been easy for the apostles to preach Christ on Good Friday, as Jesus died on the cross crying, "My God, My God, why have You forsaken Me?" But the fact that the work continued to bear fruit proves that it was from God and not from us. The Christian faith has an answer to such questions. For instance, Jesus told us about Lazarus, a poor beggar, oppressed as we were oppressed—dying, hungry, his wounds being licked by dogs—but in the end, angels took him to Abraham's bosom.

How the Underground Church Worked Partly in the Open

The Underground Church met secretly in homes, in the woods, in basements—wherever it could. As is true in many captive nations today, the Underground Church in Romania was only partially underground. Like an iceberg, a small part of its work was in the open. Under the Communists, we devised a plan of having street preaching, which in time became very risky, but by this means we reached many souls we could not reach otherwise. My wife was very active in this. Some Christians would quietly gather on a street corner and start to sing. People crowded around them to hear the beautiful singing, then my wife would deliver her message. We left the spot before the secret police arrived.

One afternoon, while I was active elsewhere, my wife delivered a message before thousands of workers at the entrance of the great MALAXA factory in the city of Bucharest. She spoke to the workers about God and salvation. The next day, many workers in this factory were shot after rebelling against the injustices of the Communists. They had heard the message just in time!

We were an Underground Church but, like John the Baptist, we spoke openly to men and rulers about Christ. Once, on the steps of one of our government buildings, two Christian brethren pushed their way to our Prime Minister, Gheorghiu Dej. In the few moments they had, they witnessed to him about Christ, urging him to turn from his sins and persecution. He had them thrown into prison for their daring witness. Years later, when Prime Minister Dej was very sick, the seed of the gospel, which they had planted years ago and for which they had suffered greatly, bore fruit. In his hour of need, the Prime Minister remembered the words that had been spoken to him. Those words were, as the Bible says, "living and powerful, and sharper than any two-edged sword" (Hebrews 4:12). They cut through the hardness of his heart and he surrendered his life to Christ. He confessed his sins, accepted the Savior, and began to serve Him in his sickness. Not long afterward he died, but went to his newfound Savior all because two Christians were willing to pay the price. And they are typical of the courageous Christians in captive nations today.

Sharing the gospel became more difficult under the Communist oppression, but we succeeded in printing several Christian pamphlets, passing them through the severe censorship of the Communists. We presented to the censor booklets that had on the front page a picture of Karl Marx, the founder of communism, and titles such as *Religion is the Opium of the People*. He considered them to be Communist publications and put the seal of approval on them. In these booklets, after a few pages full of quotations from Marx, Lenin, and Stalin—which pleased the censor—we gave our message about Christ.

We then went to the Communist demonstrations and distributed these "Communist" booklets. The Communists, seeing the picture of Marx, competed with each other to buy them. By the time they reached page ten and discovered that they were all about God and Jesus, we were far away.

Thus, the Underground Church worked not only in the secret meetings and clandestine activities, but boldly in the open proclaiming the gospel on the Communist streets and to Communist leaders. There was a price, but we were prepared to pay it. And the Underground Church is still prepared to pay it today.

Working Undercover

The secret police greatly persecuted the Underground Church, because they recognized in it the only effective resistance left. It was just the kind of resistance (a spiritual resistance) that, if left unhindered, would undermine their atheistic power. They recognized, as only the devil can, an immediate threat to them. *They knew that if a man believed in Christ, he would never be a mindless, willing subject. They knew they could imprison the physical body, but they couldn't imprison a man's spirit—his faith in God.* And so they fought very hard.

But the Underground Church also has its sympathizers or members even in the Communist governments and in the secret police.

We instructed Christians to join the secret police and put on the most hated and despised uniform in our country, so they could report the activities of the secret police to the Underground Church. Several brethren of the Underground Church did this, keeping their faith hidden. It was difficult for them to be despised by family and friends for wearing the Communist uniform and not reveal their true mission. Yet they did, so great was their love for Christ.

When I was kidnapped by police and kept imprisoned for years in strictest secrecy, a Christian doctor actually became a member of the secret police to learn my whereabouts! As a secret police doctor, he had access to the cells of all prisoners and hoped to find me. All of his friends shunned him, thinking he had become a Communist. To go around dressed in the uniform of the torturers is a much greater sacrifice than to wear the uniform of a prisoner.

The doctor found me in a deep, dark cell and sent word that I was alive. He was the first friend to discover me during my initial eight-and-a-half years in prison! Due to him, word was spread that I was alive and, when prisoners were released during the Eisenhower-Khrushchev "thaw" in 1956, Christians clamored for my release and I was freed for a short time. If it had not been for this doctor, who joined the secret police specifically to find me, I would never have been released. I would still be in prison—or in a grave—today.

Using their position in the secret police, these members of the Underground Church warned us many times and were of tremendous help. The Underground Church in Communist countries has men in the secret police today who protect and warn Christians of impending danger. Some are high up in government circles, keeping their faith in Christ secret and helping us greatly. One day in heaven they can publicly proclaim Christ, whom they serve secretly now.

Nevertheless, many members of the Underground Church were discovered and imprisoned. We had our "Judases," too, who reported our activities to the secret police. Using beatings, druggings, threats, and blackmail, the Communists tried to find ministers and laymen who would report on their brethren.

Chapter 2

"Greater Love Hath No Man ..."

I worked in both an official and underground manner until February 29, 1948. On that beautiful Sunday, on my way to church, I was kidnapped from the street by the secret police.

I had often wondered what was meant by "man-stealing," which is mentioned several times in the Bible. Communism has taught us.

Many at that time were kidnapped like this. A van of the secret police stopped in front of me, two men jumped out and pushed me into the vehicle. I was taken to a prison where I was kept secretly for over eight years. During that time, no one knew whether I was alive or dead. My wife was visited by the secret police who posed as released fellow-prisoners. They told her that they had attended my burial. She was heartbroken.

Thousands of believers from churches of all denominations were sent to prison at that time. Not only were clergymen put in jail, but also simple peasants, young boys and girls who witnessed for their faith. The prisons were full, and in Romania, as in all Communist countries, to be in prison means to be tortured.

The tortures were sometimes horrible. I prefer not to speak too much about those through which I have passed; it is too painful. When I do, I cannot sleep at night.

In the book *In God's Underground*, I recount many details of our experiences with God in jail.

Unspeakable Tortures

A pastor by the name of Florescu was tortured with red-hot iron pokers and with knives. He was beaten very badly. Then starving rats were driven into his cell through a large pipe. He could not sleep because he had to defend himself all the time. If he rested a moment, the rats would attack him.

He was forced to stand for two weeks, day and night. The Communists wished to compel him to betray his brethren, but he resisted steadfastly. Eventually, they brought his fourteen-year-old son to the prison and began to whip the boy in front of his father, saying that they would continue to beat him until the pastor said what they wished him to say. The poor man was half mad. He bore it as long as he could, then he cried to his son, "Alexander, I must say what they want! I can't bear your beating anymore!" The son answered, "Father, don't do me the injustice of having a traitor as a parent. Withstand! If they kill me, I will die with the words, 'Jesus and my fatherland.'" The Communists, enraged, fell upon the child and beat him to death, with blood spattered over the walls of the cell. He died praising God. Our dear brother Florescu was never the same after seeing this.

Handcuffs with sharp nails on the insides were placed on our wrists. If we were totally still, they didn't cut us. But in the bitterly cold cells, when we shook with cold, our wrists would be torn by the nails.

Christians were hung upside-down on ropes and beaten so severely that their bodies swung back and forth under the blows. Christians were also placed in ice-box "refrigerator cells," which were so cold that frost and ice covered the inside. I was thrown into one while I had very little clothing on. Prison doctors would watch through an opening until they saw symptoms of freezing to death, then they would give a signal and guards would rush in to take us out and make us warm. When we were finally warmed, we would immediately be put back into the ice-box cells to freeze. Thawing out, then freezing to within minutes of death, then being thawed out—over and over again! Even today there are times when I can't bear to open a refrigerator.

We Christians were sometimes forced to stand in wooden boxes only slightly larger than we were. This left no room to move. Dozens of sharp nails were driven into every side of the box, with their razor-sharp points sticking through the wood. While we stood perfectly still, it was all right. But we were forced to stand in these boxes for endless hours; when we became fatigued and swayed with tiredness, the nails would pierce our bodies. If we moved or twitched a muscle—there were the horrible nails.

What the Communists have done to Christians surpasses any possibility of human understanding. I have seen Communists whose faces while torturing believers shone with rapturous joy. They cried out while torturing the Christians, "We are the devil!"

We wrestle not against flesh and blood, but against the principalities and powers of evil. We saw that communism is not from men but from the devil. It is a spiritual force—a force of evil—and can only be countered by a greater spiritual force, the Spirit of God.

I often asked the torturers, "Don't you have pity in your hearts?" They usually answered with quotations from Lenin: "You cannot make omelets without breaking the shells of eggs," and "You cannot cut wood without making chips fly." I said again, "I know these quotations from Lenin. But there is a difference. When you cut a piece of wood it feels nothing. But here you are dealing with human beings. Every beating produces pain and there are mothers who weep." It was in vain. They are materialists. For them nothing besides matter exists and to them a man is like wood, like an eggshell. With this belief they sink to unthinkable depths of cruelty.

The cruelty of atheism is hard to believe. When a man has no faith in the reward of good or the punishment of evil, there is no reason to be human. There is no restraint from the depths of evil that is in man. The Communist torturers often said, "There is no God, no hereafter, no punishment for evil. We can do what we wish." I heard one torturer say, "I thank God, in whom I don't believe, that I have lived to this hour when I can express all the evil in my heart." He expressed it in unbelievable brutality and torture inflicted on prisoners.

I am very sorry if a crocodile eats a man, but I can't reproach the crocodile. It is not a moral being. So no reproaches can be made to the Communists. Communism has destroyed any moral sense in them. They boasted that they had no pity in their hearts.

I learned from them. As they allowed no place for Jesus in their hearts, I decided I would leave not the smallest place for Satan in mine.

I have testified before the Internal Security Subcommittee of the U.S. Senate. There I described awful things, such as Christians tied to crosses for four days and nights. The crosses were placed on the floor and hundreds of prisoners had to fulfill their bodily necessities over the faces and bodies of the crucified ones. Then the crosses were erected again and the Communists jeered and mocked: "Look at your Christ! How beautiful he is! What fragrance he brings from heaven!" I described how, after being driven nearly insane with tortures, a priest was forced to consecrate human excrement and urine and give Holy Communion to Christians in this form. This happened in the Romanian prison of Pitesti. I asked the priest afterward why he did not prefer to die rather than participate in this mockery. He answered, "Don't judge me, please! I have suffered more than Christ!" All the biblical descriptions of hell and the pains of Dante's *Inferno* are nothing in comparison with the tortures in Communist prisons.

This is only a very small part of what happened on one Sunday and on many other Sundays in the prison of Pitesti. Other things simply cannot be told. My heart would fail if I should tell them again and again. They are too terrible and obscene to put in writing. That is what your brothers in Christ went through and go through now!

If I were to continue to tell all the horrors of Communist tortures and all the self-sacrifices of Christians, I would never finish. Not only were the tortures known, but the heroic deeds were known also. The heroic examples of those in prison greatly inspired the brethren who were still free.

One of the really great heroes of the faith was Pastor Milan Haimovici.

The prisons were overcrowded and the guards did not know us by name. They called out for those who had been sentenced to get twenty-five lashes with a whip for having broken some prison rule. Innumerable times, Pastor Haimovici went to get the beating in the place of someone else. By this he won the respect of other prisoners not only for himself, but also for Christ whom he represented.

One of our workers in the Underground Church was a young girl. The Communist police discovered that she secretly spread Gospels and taught children about Christ. They decided to arrest her. But to make the arrest as agonizing and painful as they could, they decided to delay her arrest a few weeks, until the day she was to be married. On her wedding day, the girl was dressed as a bride—the most wonderful, joyous day in a girl's life! Suddenly, the door burst open and the secret police rushed in.

When the bride saw the secret police, she held out her arms toward them to be handcuffed. They roughly put the manacles on her wrists. She looked toward her beloved, then kissed the chains and said, "I thank my heavenly Bridegroom for this jewel

He has presented to me on my marriage day. I thank Him that I am worthy to suffer for Him." She was dragged off, with weeping Christians and a weeping bridegroom left behind. They knew what happens to young Christian girls in the hands of Communist guards. Her bridegroom faithfully waited for her. After five years she was released—a destroyed, broken woman, looking thirty years older. She said it was the least she could do for her Christ. Such beautiful Christians are in the Underground Church.

Resisting Brainwashing

Westerners have probably heard about brainwashing in the Korean and Vietnam Wars. I have passed through brainwashing myself. It is the most horrible torture.

We had to sit for seventeen hours a day—for weeks, months, and years—hearing:

Communism is good!
Communism is good!
Communism is good!
Christianity is stupid!
Christianity is stupid!
Christianity is stupid!
Give up!
Give up!
Give up!

Several Christians have asked me how we could resist brainwashing. There is only one method of resistance to brainwashing: it is "heart washing." If the heart is cleansed by the love of Jesus Christ, and if the heart loves Him, one can resist all tortures. What would a loving bride not do for a loving bridegroom? What would a loving mother not do for her child? If you love Christ as Mary did, who had Christ as a baby in her arms, if you love Jesus as a bride loves her bridegroom, then you can resist such tortures.

God will judge us not according to how much we endured, but how much we could love. The Christians who suffered for their faith in prisons could love. I am a witness that they could love God and men.

The tortures and brutality continued without interruption. When I lost consciousness or became too dazed to give the torturers any further hopes of confession, I would be returned to my cell. There I would lie, untended and half dead, to regain a little strength so they could work on me again. Many died at this stage, but somehow my strength always managed to return. In the ensuing years, in several different prisons, they broke four vertebrae in my back, and many other bones. They carved me in a dozen places. They burned and cut eighteen holes in my body.

When my family and I were ransomed out of Romania and brought to Norway, doctors in Oslo, seeing all this and the scars in my lungs from tuberculosis, declared that my being alive today is a pure miracle! According to their medical books, I should have been dead for years. I know myself that it is a miracle. God is a God of miracles.

I believe God performed this wonder so that you could hear my voice crying out on behalf of the Underground Church in persecuted countries. He allowed one to come out alive and cry aloud the message of your suffering, faithful brethren.

Brief Freedom—Then Re-Arrest

The year 1956 arrived. I had been in prison eight-and-a-half years. I had lost much weight, gained ugly scars, been brutally beaten and kicked, derided, starved, pressured, questioned *ad nauseum*, threatened, and neglected. None of this had produced the results my captors were seeking. So, in discouragement—and amid protests over my imprisonment—they turned me loose.

I was allowed to return to my old position as pastor for just one week. I preached two sermons. Then they called me in and told me that I could not preach anymore, nor engage in any further religious activity. What had I said? I had counseled my parishioners to have "patience, patience, and more patience." "This means you are telling them to be patient and the Americans will come and deliver them," the police shouted at me. I had also said that the wheel turns and times change. "You are telling them the Communists will not continue to rule! These are counterrevolutionary lies!" they screamed. So that was the end of my public ministry.

Probably the authorities believed that I would be afraid to defy them and continue with underground witnessing. That was where they were wrong. Secretly, and with my family's support, I returned to the work I had been doing before.

Again I witnessed to hidden groups of the faithful, coming and going like a ghost under the protection of those who could be trusted. This time I had scars to corroborate my message about the evil of the atheist viewpoint and to encourage faltering souls to trust God and be brave. I directed a secret network of evangelists who helped each other spread the gospel under providentially blinded Communist eyes. After all, if a man can be so blind as to not see the hand of God at work, perhaps he will not see that of an evangelist either.

Eventually, the ceaseless interest of the police in my activities and whereabouts paid off for them. Again I was discovered and imprisoned. For some reason they did not imprison my family this time, perhaps because of all the publicity I had received. I had had eight-and-a-half years of prison and then a couple years of relative freedom. Now I was to be imprisoned for five-and-a-half years more.

My second imprisonment was in many ways worse than the first. I knew well what to expect. My physical condition became very bad almost immediately. But we continued the work of the Underground Church where we could—in Communist prisons.

We Made a Deal: We Preached and They Beat

It was strictly forbidden to preach to other prisoners, as it is in captive nations today. It was understood that whoever was caught doing this received a severe beating. A number of us decided to pay the price for the privilege of preaching, so we accepted their terms. It was a deal: we preached and they beat us. We were happy preaching; they were happy beating us—so everyone was happy.

The following scene happened more times than I can remember. A brother was preaching to the other prisoners when the guards suddenly burst in, surprising him halfway through a phrase. They hauled him down the corridor to their "beating room." After what seemed an endless beating, they brought him back and threw him—bloody and bruised—on the prison floor. Slowly, he picked up his battered body, painfully straightened his clothing and said, "Now, brethren, where did I leave off when I was interrupted?" He continued his gospel message!

I have seen beautiful things!

Sometimes the preachers were laymen, simple men inspired by the Holy Spirit who often preached beautifully. All of their heart was in their words, for to preach under such punitive circumstances was no trifling matter. Then the guards would come and take the preacher out and beat him half to death.

In the prison of Gherla, a Christian named Grecu was sentenced to be beaten to death. The process lasted a few weeks, during which he was beaten very slowly. He would be hit once at the bottom of the feet with a rubber club, and then left. After some minutes he would again be hit, after another few minutes again. He was beaten on the testicles. Then a doctor gave him an injection. He recovered and was given very good food to restore his strength, and then he was beaten again, until he eventually died under this slow, repeated beating. One who led this torture was a member of the Central Committee of the Communist Party, whose name was Reck.

During the beatings, Reck said something to Grecu that the Communists often said to Christians, "You know, *I* am God. I have power of life and death over you. The one who is in heaven cannot decide to keep you in life. Everything depends upon *me*. If I wish, you live. If I wish, you are killed. *I am God!*" So he mocked the Christian.

Brother Grecu, in this horrible situation, gave Reck a very interesting answer, which I heard afterward from Reck himself. He said, "You don't know what a deep thing you have said. Every caterpillar is in reality a butterfly, *if it develops rightly*. You have not been created to be a torturer, a man who kills. You have been created to become like God, with the life of the Godhead in your heart. Many who have been persecutors like you, have come to realize—like the apostle Paul—that it is shameful for a man to commit atrocities, that they can do much better things. So they have become partakers of the divine nature. Jesus said to the Jews of His time, 'Ye are gods.' Believe me, Mr. Reck, your real calling is to be Godlike—to have the character of God, not a torturer."

At that moment Reck did not pay much attention to the words of his victim, as Saul of Tarsus did not pay attention to the beautiful witness of Stephen being killed in his presence. But those words worked in his heart. And Reck later understood that this was his real calling.

One great lesson arose from all the beatings, tortures, and butchery of the Communists: *that the spirit is master of the body*. We felt the torture, but it often seemed as something distant and far removed from the spirit which was lost in the glory of Christ and His presence with us.

When we were given one slice of bread a week and dirty soup every day, we decided we would faithfully "tithe" even then. Every tenth week we took the slice of bread and gave it to weaker brethren as our "tithe" to the Master.

When one Christian was sentenced to death, he was allowed to see his wife before being executed. His last words to his wife were, "You must know that I die loving those who kill me. They don't know what they do and my last request of you is to love them, too. Don't have bitterness in your heart because they killed your beloved one. We will meet in heaven." These words impressed the officer of the secret police who attended the discussion between the two. He later told me the story in prison where he had been sent for becoming a Christian.

In the Tirgu-Ocna prison was a very young prisoner named Matchevici. He had been put in prison at the age of eighteen. Because of the tortures, he was very sick with tuberculosis. His family found out somehow that he was in this grave state of health and sent him one hundred bottles of streptomycin, which could make the difference between life and death. The political officer of the prison called Matchevici and showed him the parcel and said, "Here is the medicine that can save your life. But you are not allowed to receive parcels from your family. Personally, I would like to help you. You are young. I would not like you to die in prison. Help me to be able to help you! Give me information against your fellow prisoners and this will enable me to justify before my superiors why I gave you the parcel."

Matchevici answered, "I don't wish to remain alive and be ashamed to look in a mirror, because I will see the face of a traitor. I cannot accept such a condition. I prefer to die." The officer of the secret police shook Matchevici's hand and said, "I congratulate you. I didn't expect any other answer from you. But I would like to make another proposal. Some of the prisoners have become our informers. They claim to be Communist and they are denouncing you. They play a double role. We have no confidence in them. We would like to know in what measure they are sincere. Toward you they are traitors who are doing you much harm, informing us about your words and deeds. I understand that you don't want to betray your comrades. But give us information about those who oppose you so you will save your life!" Matchevici answered, as promptly as the first time, "I am a disciple of Christ and He has taught us to love even our enemies. The men who betray us do us much harm but I *cannot* reward evil with evil. I cannot give information even against them. I pity them. I pray for them. I don't wish to have any connection with the Communists." Matchevici came back from the discussion with the political officer and died in the same cell I was in. I saw him die—he was praising God. Love conquered even the natural thirst for life.

If a poor man is a great lover of music, he gives his last dollar to listen to a concert. He is then without money, but he does not feel frustrated. He has heard beautiful things. I don't feel frustrated to have lost many years in prison. I have seen beautiful things. I myself have been among the weak and insignificant ones in prison, but have had the privilege to be in the same jail with great saints, heroes of faith who equaled the Christians of the first centuries. They went gladly to die for Christ. The spiritual beauty of such saints and heroes of faith can never be described.

The things that I say here are not exceptional. The supernatural things have become natural to Christians in the Underground Church who have returned to their first love.

Before entering prison, I loved Christ very much. Now, after having seen the Bride of Christ (His spiritual Body) in prison, I would say that I love the Underground Church almost as much as I love Christ Himself. I have seen her beauty, her spirit of sacrifice.

What Happened to My Wife and Son?

I was taken away from my wife and I did not know what had happened to her. Only after many years I learned that she had been put in prison, too. Christian women suffer much more than men in prison. Girls have been raped by brutal guards. The mockery, the obscenity, is horrible. The women were forced to work at hard labor building a canal, fulfilling the same workload as men. They shoveled earth in winter. Prostitutes were made overseers and competed in torturing the faithful. My wife has eaten grass like cattle to stay alive. Hungry prisoners ate rats and snakes at this canal. One of the joys of the guards on Sundays was to throw women into the Danube and then fish them out, to laugh about them, to mock them about their wet bodies, to throw them back and fish them out again. My wife was thrown in the Danube in this manner.

My son was left to wander on the street when his mother and father were taken away. Mihai had been very religious from childhood and very interested in matters of faith. At the age of nine, when his parents were taken away from him, he passed through a crisis in his Christian life. He became bitter and questioned all of his religion. He had problems that children usually don't have at this age. He had to think about earning his living.

It was a crime to help families of Christian martyrs. Two ladies who helped him were arrested and beaten so badly that they were permanently crippled. A lady who risked her life and took Mihai into her house was sentenced to eight years in prison for the crime of having helped families of prisoners. All of her teeth were kicked out and her bones were broken. She will never be able to work again. She, too, will be a cripple for life.

"Mihai, Believe in Jesus!"

At the age of eleven, Mihai began to earn his living as a regular worker. Suffering had produced a wavering in his faith. But after two years of Sabina's imprisonment he was allowed to see her. He went to the Communist prison and saw his mother behind iron bars. She was dirty, thin, with calloused hands, wearing the shabby uniform of a prisoner. He scarcely recognized her. Her first words were, "Mihai, believe in Jesus!" The guards, in a savage rage, pulled her away from Mihai and took her out. Mihai wept seeing his mother dragged away. This minute was the minute of his conversion. He knew that if Christ can be loved under such circumstances, He surely is the true Savior. He said afterward, "If Christianity had no other arguments in its favor than the fact that my mother believes in it, this is enough for me." That was the day he fully accepted Christ.

In school, he had a continuous battle for existence. He was a good pupil and as a reward he was given a red necktie—a sign of membership in the Young Communist Pioneers. My son said, "I will never wear the necktie of those who put my father and mother in prison." He was expelled from school for this. After having lost a year, he entered school again, hiding the fact that he was the son of Christian prisoners.

Later, he had to write a thesis against the Bible. In this thesis he wrote: "The arguments against the Bible are weak and the quotations against the Bible are untrue. Surely the professor has not read the Bible. The Bible is in harmony with science." Again he was expelled. This time he had to lose two school years.

In the end he was allowed to study in the seminary. Here he was taught "Marxist theology." Everything was explained according to the pattern of Karl Marx. Mihai protested publicly in class, and other students joined him. The result was that he was expelled and could not finish his theological studies.

Once in school, when a professor delivered an atheistic speech, my son rose and contradicted the professor, telling him what responsibility he took upon himself by leading so many young men astray. The entire class took his side. It was necessary that one should have the courage to speak out first, then all the others were on his side. To get an education he constantly tried to hide the fact that he was the son of Wurmbrand, a Christian prisoner. But often it was discovered and again there was the familiar scene of being called to the school director's office and being expelled.

Mihai also suffered much from hunger. Many families of jailed Christians in Communist countries nearly starve to death. It is a great crime to help them.

I will tell you just one case of suffering of a family that I know personally. A brother entered prison on account of his work in the Underground Church. He left behind a wife with six children. His older daughters of seventeen and nineteen could not get a job. The only one that gives jobs in a Communist country is the state, and it does not give jobs to children of "criminal" Christians. Please don't judge this story according to moral standards; just receive the facts.

The two daughters of a Christian martyr—Christians themselves—became prostitutes to support their younger brothers and sick mother. Their younger brother of fourteen became insane when he saw it and had to be put in an asylum. When years later the imprisoned father returned, his only prayer was, "God, take me to prison again. I cannot bear to see this." His prayer was answered and he was jailed again for the crime of having witnessed for Christ to children. His daughters were no longer prostitutes, as they received jobs by complying with the demands of the secret police—they became informers. As daughters of a Christian martyr, they are received with honor in every house. They listen and then they report everything they hear to the secret police.

Don't just say that this is ugly and immoral—of course it is—but *ask yourself if it is not also your sin that such tragedies occur*, that such Christian families are left alone, and are not helped by you who are free.

Chapter 3

Ransom and Release for Work in the West

A total of fourteen years in prison passed for me. During all this time I never saw a Bible or any other book. I had forgotten how to write. Because of the starvation, drugging, and tortures, I had forgotten the Holy Scriptures. But on the day that I fulfilled fourteen years, out of oblivion came into my mind the verse: "So Jacob served seven years for Rachel, and they seemed but a few days to him because of the love he had for her" (Genesis 29:20). Very soon after this I was released through a general amnesty given in our country, very much under the influence of American public opinion.

I saw my wife again. She had waited faithfully for me for fourteen years. We began our new life in poverty, because those who are arrested have everything taken from them.

The priests and pastors who were released were allowed to have small churches. A church in the town of Orsova was given to me. The Communist Department of Cults told me it had thirty-five members in it and warned that it must never have thirty-six! I was also told that I must be their agent and report to the secret police on every member and keep all youth away. This is how the Communists use churches as their "tool" of control.

I knew that if I preached, many would come to hear. So I never tried even to begin working in the official church. Instead, I ministered again in the Underground Church, sharing all the beauties and the dangers of this work.

During the years I was imprisoned, God had moved wonderfully. The Underground Church was no longer abandoned and forgotten. Americans and other Christians had begun to help us and pray for us.

One afternoon as I rested in the house of a brother in a provincial town, he awoke me and said, "Brethren from abroad have come." In the West there were Christians who had not forgotten or abandoned us. Rank-and-file Christians had organized a secret work of relief for families of Christian martyrs, and were smuggling in Christian literature and help.

In the other room I found six brethren who had come to do this work. After speaking with me at length, they told me that they had heard that at this address there was someone who had spent fourteen years in prison, and they would like to see him. I told them that I was the man. They said, "We expected to see someone melancholic. You cannot be this person because you are full of joy." I assured them that I was the imprisoned one and my joy was in knowing that they had come and that we were no longer forgotten. Steady, regular help began to come to the Underground Church. By secret channels we got many Bibles and other Christian literature, as well as relief for families of Christian martyrs. Now, with their help, we of the Underground Church could work much better.

It was not only that they gave us the Word of God, but we saw that we were beloved. They brought us a word of comfort. During the years of brainwashing, we had heard, "Nobody loves you anymore, nobody loves you anymore, nobody loves you anymore." Now we saw American and English Christians who risked their lives to show us that they loved us. We later helped them develop a technique of secret work, so they could creep undetected into houses surrounded by the secret police.

The value of the Bibles smuggled in by these means cannot be understood by an American or an English Christian who "swims" in Bibles.

My family and I would not have survived without the material help I received from praying Christians abroad. The same is true with many other underground pastors and martyrs in Communist countries. I can testify out of my own experience about the material and even greater moral help that has been given to us by special missions formed for this purpose in the free world. For us, these believers were like angels sent by God!

Because of the renewed work of the Underground Church, I was in very great danger of still another arrest. At this time, two Christian organizations, the Norwegian Mission to the Jews and the Hebrew Christian Alliance, paid the Communist government a ransom of $10,000 for me—over five times the standard price for a political prisoner. I could now leave Romania.

Why I Left Communist Romania

I would not have left Romania, despite the dangers, if the leaders of the Underground Church had not commanded me to use this opportunity to leave the country, to be the "voice" of the Underground Church to the free world. They wished me to speak to you of the Western world on their behalf about their sufferings and needs. I came to the West, but my heart remained with them. I would never have left Romania if I had not understood the great necessity for you to hear of the sufferings and the courageous work of the Underground Church, but this is my mission.

Before leaving Romania, I was called twice to the secret police. They told me that the money had been received for me. (Romania sells its citizens for money, because of the economic crisis that communism has brought to our country.) They told me, "Go to the West and preach Christ as much as you like, but don't touch us! Don't speak a word against us! We tell you frankly what we plan for you if you do tell what happened. First of all, for $1,000 we can find a gangster to kill you, or we can kidnap you." (I have been in the same cell with an Orthodox bishop, Vasile Leul, who had been kidnapped in Austria and brought to Romania. All of his fingernails were torn out. I have been with others from Berlin. Romanians have even been kidnapped from Italy and Paris.) They told me further, "We can also destroy you morally by spreading a story about you with a girl, theft, or some sin of your youth. The Westerners—especially Americans—are very easily deceived."

Having threatened me, they allowed me to come to the West. They had great confidence in the brainwashing through which I passed. In the West, there are now many who have passed through the same things as I, but who are silent. Some of them have even praised communism after having been tortured by the Communists. The Communists were very sure that I, too, would be silent.

So in December 1965, my family and I were allowed to leave Romania.

My last deed before leaving was to go to the grave of the colonel who had given the order for my arrest and who had ordered my years of torture. I placed a flower on his grave. By doing this I dedicated myself to bringing the joys of Christ that I have to the Communists who are so empty spiritually.

I hate the Communist system but I love the men. I hate the sin but I love the sinner. I love the Communists with all of my heart. Communists can kill Christians but they cannot kill their love toward even those who killed them. I have not the slightest bitterness or resentment against the Communists or my torturers.

Chapter 4

Defeating Communism with the Love of Christ

The Jews have a legend that, when their forefathers were saved from Egypt and the Egyptians drowned in the Red Sea, the angels joined the songs of triumph sung by the Israelites. And God said to the angels, "The Jews are men and can rejoice about their escape. But from you I expect more understanding. Are the Egyptians not also my creatures? Do I not love them, too? How do you fail to feel my sorrow about their tragic fate?"

Joshua 5:13 says, "And it came to pass, when Joshua was by Jericho, that he lifted his eyes and looked, and behold, a Man stood opposite him with His sword drawn in His hand. And Joshua went to Him and said to Him, 'Are You for us or for our adversaries?'"

If the one met by Joshua had been only a man, the answer could have been "I am for you" or "I am for your adversaries," or even "I am neutral." These are the only possible human responses to such a question. But the Being whom Joshua met was sent from the Lord and, therefore, when asked whether He was for or against

Israel, gave an answer that is the most unexpected and difficult to understand: "No." What does this "no" mean?

He came from a place where beings are not for or against, but where everyone and everything are understood, looked upon with pity and compassion, and loved with fire.

There is a human level on which communism must be utterly fought against. On this level we have to fight against Communists, too, they being the supporters of this cruel, savage ideal.

But Christians are more than mere men; they are children of God, partakers of the divine nature. Therefore, tortures endured in Communist prisons have not made me hate Communists. They are God's creatures; how can I hate them? But neither can I be their friend. Friendship means one soul in two breasts. I am not one soul with the Communists. They hate the notion of God. I love God.

If I were asked, "Are you for the Communists or against them?" my answer would be a complex one. Communism is one of the greatest menaces to mankind. I am utterly opposed to it and wish to fight it until it is overthrown. But, in the spirit, I am seated in heavenly places with Jesus. I am seated in the sphere of the "no," in which, notwithstanding all of their crimes, the Communists are understood and loved, a sphere in which there are angelic beings trying to help everyone attain the highest goal of human life, which is to become Christlike. Therefore, my aim is to spread the gospel to the Communists, to give them the good news about Christ, who is my Lord and loves the Communists. He has said Himself that He loves every man and that He would rather leave ninety-nine righteous sheep than allow the one that went astray to remain lost. His apostles and all the great teachers of Christianity have taught this universal love in His name. St. Macary said, "If a man loves all men passionately, but says only about one man that him he cannot love, the man who says this is no more a Christian, because his love is not all-embracing." St. Augustine teaches, "If all mankind had been righteous and only one man a sinner, Christ would have come to endure the same cross for this one man, He so loves every individual." The Christian teaching is clear. Communists are men and Christ loves them. So does every man who has the mind of Christ. We love the sinner even though we hate the sin.

We know about the love of Christ toward the Communists by our own love toward them.

I have seen Christians in Communist prisons with fifty pounds of chains on their feet, tortured with red-hot iron pokers, in whose throats spoonfuls of salt had been forced, being kept afterward without water, starving, whipped, suffering from cold—and praying with fervor for the Communists. This is humanly inexplicable! It is the love of Christ, which was poured out in our hearts.

Later, the Communists who had tortured us were sent to prison, too. Under communism, Communists, and even Communist rulers, are put in prison almost as often as their adversaries. Now the tortured and the torturer were in the same cell. And while the non-Christians showed hatred toward their former inquisitors and beat them, Christians took their defense, even at the risk of being beaten themselves and accused of being accomplices with communism. I have seen Christians give away their last slice of bread (we were given one slice a week) and the medicine that could save their lives to a sick Communist torturer, who was now a fellow prisoner.

These are the last words of Iuliu Maniu, a Christian and the former Prime Minister of Romania, who died in prison: "If the Communists are overthrown in our country, it will be the most holy duty of every Christian to go into the streets and at the risk of his own life defend the Communists from the righteous fury of the multitudes whom they have tyrannized."

In the first days after my conversion, I felt that I would not be able to live any longer. Walking on the street, I felt a physical pain for every man and woman who passed by. It was like a knife in my heart, so burning was the question of whether or not he or she was saved. If a member of the congregation sinned, I would weep for hours. The longing for the salvation of all souls has remained in my heart and the Communists are not excluded from it.

In solitary confinement, we could not pray as before. We were unimaginably hungry; we had been drugged until we acted like idiots. We were as weak as skeletons. The Lord's Prayer was much too long for us—we could not concentrate enough to say it. My only prayer repeated again and again was, "Jesus, I love You."

And then, one glorious day I got the answer from Jesus: "You love me? Now I will show you how I love you." At once, I felt a flame in my heart, which burned like the coronal streamers of the sun. The disciples on the way to Emmaus said that their hearts burned when Jesus spoke with them. So it was with me. I knew the love of the One who gave His life on the cross for us all. Such love cannot exclude the Communists, however grave their sins.

Communists have committed and still commit horrors but "love is as strong as death, jealousy as cruel as the grave ... Many waters cannot quench love, nor can the floods drown it" (Song of Solomon 8:6,7). As the grave insists on having all—rich and poor; young and old; men of all races, nations, and political convictions; saints and criminals—so love is all-embracing. Christ, the Incarnate Love, wants all men to come to Him, including the Communists.

A minister who had been horribly beaten was thrown into my cell. He was half-dead, with blood streaming from his face and body. We washed him. Some prisoners cursed the Communists. Groaning, he said, "Please, don't curse them! Keep silent! I wish to pray for them."

How We Could Be Joyful—Even in Prison

When I look back on my fourteen years in prison, it was occasionally a very happy time. Other prisoners and even the guards very often wondered at how happy Christians could be under the most terrible circumstances. We could not be prevented from singing, although we were beaten for this. I imagine that nightingales, too, would sing, even if they knew that after finishing they would be killed for it. Christians in prison danced for joy. How could they be so happy under such tragic conditions?

I meditated often in prison about Jesus' words to His disciples, "Blessed are the eyes which see the things you see" (Luke 10:23). The disciples had just come back from a tour through Palestine where they had seen horrors. Palestine was an oppressed country.

Everywhere there was the terrible misery of a tyrannized people. The disciples met sickness, plagues, hunger, and sorrow. They entered houses from which patriots had been taken to prison, leaving behind weeping parents or wives. It was not a beautiful world to look upon.

Still Jesus said, "Blessed are the eyes which see the things you see." That was because they had not seen only the suffering. They had also seen the Savior. For the first time a few ugly worms—caterpillars that creep on leaves—understood that, after this miserable existence, there comes life as a beautiful, multicolored butterfly, able to flit from flower to flower. This happiness was ours, too.

Around me were "Jobs"—some much more afflicted than Job had been. But I knew the end of Job's story, how he received twice as much as he had before. I had around me men like Lazarus the beggar, hungry and covered with boils. But I knew that angels would take these men to the bosom of Abraham. I saw them as they will be in the future. I saw in the shabby, dirty, weak martyr near me the splendidly crowned saint of tomorrow.

But looking at men like this—not as they are, but as they will be—I could also see in our persecutors a Saul of Tarsus—a future apostle Paul. And some have already become so. Many officers of the secret police to whom we witnessed became Christians and were happy to later suffer in prison for having found our Christ. Although we were whipped, as Paul was, in our jailers we saw the potential of the jailer in Philippi who became a convert. We dreamed that soon they would ask, "What must I do to be saved?" In those who mocked the Christians who were tied to crosses and smeared with excrement, we saw the crowd of Golgotha who were soon to beat their breasts in fear of having sinned.

It was in prison that we found the hope of salvation for the Communists. It was there that we developed a sense of responsibility toward them. It was in being tortured by them that we learned to love them.

A great part of my family was murdered. It was in my own house that their murderer was converted. It was also the most suitable place. So in Communist prisons the idea of a Christian mission to the Communists was born.

God sees things differently than we see them, just as we see differently than an ant. From the human point of view, to be tied to a cross and smeared with excrement is a horrible thing. Nonetheless, the Bible calls the sufferings of martyrs "light afflictions." To be in prison for fourteen years is a long period to us. The Bible calls it "but for a moment," and tells us that these things are "working for us a far more exceeding and eternal weight of glory" (2 Corinthians 4:17). This gives us the right to suppose that the fierce crimes of the Communists, which are inexcusable to us, are lighter in the eyes of God than they are in our eyes. Their tyranny, which has lasted almost an entire century, may be before God, for whom a thousand years are like one day, only a moment of erring astray. They still have the possibility of being saved.

The gates of heaven are not closed for the Communists. Neither is the light quenched for them. They can repent like everyone else. And we must call them to repentance.

Only love can change the Communist and the terrorist (a love that must be clearly distinguished from compromise with non-Christian philosophies, practiced by many church leaders). Hatred blinds. Hitler was an anti-Communist, but one who hated. Therefore, instead of conquering them, he helped them win one-third of the world.

With love we planned a missionary work among the Communists in prison. And thereby we thought first of all about the Communist rulers.

Some mission directors seem to have studied little church history. How was Norway won for Christ? By winning King Olaf. Russia first had the gospel when its king, Vladimir, was won. Hungary was won by winning St. Stephen, its king. The same with Poland. In Africa, where the chief of the tribe has been won, the tribe follows. We set up missions to rank-and-file men who may become very fine Christians, but who have little influence and cannot change the state of things.

We must win rulers, leaders in politics, economics, science, and the arts. They mold the souls of men. Winning them, you win the people they lead and influence.

From the missionary point of view, communism has an advantage over other social systems in that it is more centralized. If the President of the U.S. were converted to Mormonism, America would not become Mormon because of it. But if Communist government leaders were converted to Christianity, perhaps their whole country could be reached. So great is the impact of leaders.

Can these leaders be converted? Surely, because they are unhappy and insecure just like their victims. Nearly all the Communist rulers of Russia ended in prison or were shot by their own comrades. The same in China. Even the ministers of the interior like Iagoda, Yezhov, Beria, who seemed to have all power in hand, ended just like the last counterrevolutionary: with a bullet in the neck. Years ago, Shelepin, the Minister of the Interior of the Soviet Union, and Rankovic, the Minister of the Interior of Yugoslavia, were thrown out like dirty rags.

How We Can Attack Communism Spiritually

The Communist regime makes no one happy, not even its profiteers. Even they tremble that any night the van of the secret police may take them away because the party line has changed.

I have known many Communist leaders personally. They are heavily-laden men, and only Jesus can give them rest.

To win Communist rulers for Christ may mean to save the world from nuclear destruction, to save mankind from hunger because so much of its revenues now go to costly armaments. To win the Communist rulers may mean the end of international tension. To win the Communist rulers will mean to fill Christ and the angels with joy. Many other areas in which missionaries labor so hard, such as New Guinea or Madagascar, may follow simply if the Communist rulers are won, because this will give Christianity an entirely new impetus.

I have personally known converted Communists. I myself was a militant atheist in my youth. Converted atheists and Communists love Christ much, because they have sinned very much.

Strategic thought is needed in missionary work. From the point of view of salvation, all souls are equal; from the point of view of missionary strategy, they are not equal. It is more important to win a man of great influence, who can afterward win thousands, than to speak to a savage in the jungle assuring salvation only for him. Therefore, Jesus chose to end His ministry not in some small village, but in Jerusalem, the spiritual headquarters of the world. For this same reason, Paul strove so much to arrive in Rome.

The Bible says that the seed of the woman will bruise the head of the serpent (Genesis 3:15). We tickle the serpent on the belly, making him laugh. Today the serpent continues to crawl through China, North Korea, Vietnam, and Laos. There are nations in the Middle East where not one church building is allowed to stand. The plight of such captive nations must continually be addressed by church leaders and mission directors, as well as by every thoughtful Christian.

We must give up routine work. It is written, "Cursed is he who does the work of the Lord deceitfully" (Jeremiah 48:10). The Church must wage a frontal, spiritual attack on the principalities in captive nations. Wars are won only by offensive, never by defensive, strategy.

Psalm 107:16 says that God cuts the bars of iron in two. The Iron Curtain was a small thing for Him.

The Early Church worked secretly and illegally, and it triumphed. We must learn again to work in the same manner.

Until the Communist era, I never understood why so many persons of the New Testament are called by nicknames: Simeon who was called Niger, John called Mark, and so on. We continue to use secret names in our work in captive nations.

I never understood before why Jesus, wishing to have the last supper arranged, did not give an address but said, "Go into the city, and a man will meet you carrying a pitcher of water" (Mark 14:13). Now I understand. We also give such secret signs of recognition in the work of the Underground Church.

If we agree to work like this—to come back to the methods of early Christianity—we can work effectively for Christ in these closed countries.

But when I met some church leaders of the West, instead of love toward the Communists—which would have led long ago to the organization of a missionary work in Communist countries—I found their policy on the side of the Communists. I did not find the compassion of the Good Samaritan toward the lost souls of the house of Karl Marx.

A man really believes not what he recites in his creed, but only the things he is ready to die for. The Christians of the Underground Church have proved that they are ready to die for their faith. Our international network of missions continues today with a secret work in captive nations that can mean for them imprisonment, torture, and death if caught in such a country. I believe in the things I write.

I have the right to ask: Would the church leaders of America who make friends with communism be ready to die for their belief? Who prevents them from giving up their high positions in the West to become official pastors in the East, cooperating there—on the spot—with Communists? The proof of such a faith has not yet been given by any Western church leader.

Human words grow out of the need of men to understand each other and to express their feelings toward one another. There are no human words to express in an adequate manner the mysteries of God and the heights of spiritual life. Likewise, there are no human words that can describe the depths of devilish cruelty. Can you express in words what a man felt who was about to be thrown into a furnace by the Nazis, or who saw his child thrown into this furnace?

So it is useless to try to describe what Christians have suffered and still suffer under the Communists.

I was in prison with Lucretiu Patrascanu, the man who brought communism to power in Romania. His comrades rewarded him by putting him in jail. Though he was sane, they put him in a mental hospital with madmen, until he became mad, too. They did the same to Anna Pauker, their former Secretary of State. Christians are often given a similar type of treatment. They receive electric shocks and are put in straitjackets.

The world was horrified about what happened on the streets in China. In view of everyone, the Red Guard exercised its terror. Now try to imagine what happens to Christians in a Chinese jail, where no one else sees! I heard that when a renowned Chinese evangelical writer and other Christians refused to deny their faith, their captors cut off their ears, tongues, and legs. Christians are still in Chinese prisons today.

But the worst thing Communists do is not that they torture and kill the bodies of men. They hopelessly falsify the thoughts of men and poison the youth and the children. They have placed their men into positions of leadership in the churches to lead the Christians and to destroy the churches. They teach youth *not* to believe in God and Christ but to *hate* these names.

In what words can we express the tragedy of Christian martyrs, who, coming home after years in prison, are received with scorn by their children, who in the meantime have become militant atheists?

This book is written not so much with ink, as with the blood of bleeding hearts.

As in the book of Daniel when the three young men who were put in the furnace did not smell like fire upon being delivered from it, so the Christians who have been in Communist prisons don't smell like bitterness against the Communists.

A flower, if you bruise it under your feet, rewards you by giving you its perfume. Likewise Christians, tortured by the Communists, rewarded their torturers by love. We brought many of our jailors to Christ. And we are dominated by one desire: to give Communists who have made us suffer the best we have, the salvation that comes from our Lord Jesus Christ.

I did not have the privilege, as many of my brethren in the faith had, to die a martyr's death in prison. I was released and could even come out of Romania to the West.

In the West I found in many church leaders the contrary sentiment of that which was predominant in the Underground Church behind the Bamboo and former Iron Curtains. Many Christians in the West have no love for those in captive nations. Proof of it is that they do nothing for their salvation. They have missions to persuade Christians of one denomination to change to another. But many have no mission to captive nations, claiming that such work is "against the law"! They don't love them. Otherwise they would have long since created such an impossible-looking mission, just as William Carey who loved the Indians and Hudson Taylor the Chinese have created their respective missions.

But it is not enough that they do not love those in captive nations and do nothing to win them for Christ. By their complacency, by their neglect, and sometimes by acting as actual accomplices, some Western church leaders strengthen the infidels in their infidelity. They help the Communists to intrude into Western churches and to win leadership in the churches of the world. They help Christians remain unaware of the danger of communism.

By not loving the Communists and those from other captive nations, and by doing nothing to win them for Christ (under the pretext that they are not allowed to do so, as if the first Christians asked permission from Nero to spread the gospel), Western church leaders do not love their own flocks either, if they do not allow them to participate in this spiritual battle around the world.

The Lessons of History Are Ignored

In the first centuries, Christianity flourished in North Africa. From there came St. Augustine, St. Cyprian, St. Athanasius, and Tertullian. The Christians of North Africa neglected just one duty: to win the Muslims for Christ. The result was that the Muslims invaded North Africa and uprooted Christianity for centuries. North Africa belongs to the Muslims even now, and they are called by Christian missions "the bloc of unconvertibles." Let us learn something from history!

At the time of the Reformation, the religious interests of Huss, Luther, and Calvin coincided with the interests of the European peoples to get rid of the yoke of the Papacy, which was then an oppressive political and economic power. Likewise today, the interests of the Underground Church in spreading the gospel to tyrannical regimes and their victims coincide with the vital interest of all free peoples in continuing to live in freedom.

Many tyrants have nuclear weapons; to attack them militarily would start a new world war with hundreds of millions of victims. Many Western rulers are brainwashed and do not even wish to overthrow such rulers. They have said so frequently. They wish that drug addiction, gangsterism, cancer, and tuberculosis would disappear, but not evil systems such as communism, which has claimed far more victims than all these together.

Ilya Ehrenburg, the Soviet writer, says that if Stalin had done nothing else all of his life than to write the names of his innocent victims, his life would not have been long enough to finish the job. Khrushchev said at the Twentieth Congress of the Communist Party, "Stalin liquidated thousands of honest and guiltless Communists ... Of a hundred and thirty-nine members and candidates of the Central Committee who were chosen at the Seventeenth Congress, ninety-eight, that is seventy percent, were later arrested and shot."

Now imagine what he did to the Christians! Khrushchev disowned Stalin, but continued to do the same thing. Since 1959, half of the churches of Soviet Russia that remained open were closed.

In China, waves of barbarism rose worse than that of the Stalinist period. Open church life ceased completely. In Russia and Romania there were new arrests. (After the fall of communism in the Soviet Union, the government admitted to the mass arrests of Christians in Russia.)

With terror and deceit, in countries with one billion inhabitants, an entire generation of youth is brought up in hatred toward everything Western and especially toward Christianity.

It was not an unusual sight in Russia to see local officials stand in front of churches watching for children. Those who went to church were slapped and thrown out. The future destroyers of Western Christianity were carefully and systematically brought up!

There is only one force that can change evil governments. It is the same force that enabled Christian states to take the place of the heathen Roman Empire, the force that made Christians of savage Teutons and Vikings, the force that overthrew the bloody Inquisition. This force is the power of the gospel, represented by the Underground Church that works in all captive nations.

To sustain this Church and to help her is not only a question of unity with our suffering brethren. It means life or death for your country and for your churches. To sustain this Church is not only in the interests of free Christians, but should also be the policy of free governments. The Underground Church has already won Communist rulers to Christ. Gheorghiu Dej, Romania's Prime Minister, died a converted man after confessing his sin and changing his sinful life. In many captive nations there are members of the government who are hidden Christians. This can spread. Then we will be able to expect a real change in the policy of some governments—not changes like those of Tito and Gomulka, after which the same dictatorship of a cruel atheistic party continued—but a turn toward Christianity and freedom.

Exceptional opportunities exist now for this.

Believers in communism, who very often are as sincere in their beliefs as Christians are in theirs, are passing through a great crisis. They had really believed that communism would create a brotherhood among nations. Now they see that Communist countries have fallen apart like the Eastern Bloc countries.

They had really believed that communism would create an earthly paradise, opposed to what they call the illusory paradise in heaven. And now their peoples are hungry. Wheat has to be imported from capitalist countries. Such is the case with North Korea's famine. Considered one of the world's most isolated nations, North Korea currently stands at the brink of utter physical destruction. Floods have destroyed crops, obliterating their food supply. Now, out of desperation, North Korea has begun to crack open its windows and doors for the rest of the world to catch a glimpse of what's been kept behind barbed wire.

The Communists had believed in their leaders. Now they have read in their own newspapers that Stalin was a mass murderer and Khrushchev an idiot. The same with their national heroes like Rakosi, Gero, Anna Pauker, Rankovici, and so on. The Communists no longer believe in the infallibility of their leaders. They are like Catholics without a Pope.

There is a void in the hearts of Communists. This void can be filled by Christ alone. The human heart by nature seeks after God. There is a spiritual vacuum in every man until it is filled by Christ. This is true also for the Communists and those in other captive nations. In the gospel there is a power of love that can appeal to them, too. I have seen it happen. I know it can be done.

Christians—mocked and tortured by the Communists—have forgotten and forgiven what has been done to them personally and to their families. They do their best to help the Communists pass through the crisis and find the way to Christ. For this work they need our help.

And not only for this. Christian love is always universal. With Christians, there is no partiality. Jesus said that the sun of God rises over the good and the evil. The same is true about Christian love.

Those Christian leaders in the West who show friendship to the Communists and other tyrannical regimes justify it by the teaching of Jesus that we must love even our enemies. But never did Jesus teach that we must love *only* our enemies, forgetting our brethren.

They show their "love" by wining and dining those whose hands are full of the blood of Christians, not by giving them the good news of Christ. But those oppressed by tyrants are forgotten. They are not loved.

Decades ago, the Evangelical and Catholic churches of West Germany gave $125 million for the hungry. American Christians give even more.

There are many hungry people, but I cannot imagine anyone hungrier or more entitled to help from free Christians than Christian martyrs. If German, British, American, and Scandinavian churches raise so much money for relief, it should go for everyone in need, but first for the Christian martyrs and their families.

Does it happen so now?

I was ransomed by Christian organizations, which proves that Christians can be ransomed. However, I may be the only case of someone ransomed from Romania by Christians. And the fact of my ransom will accuse Christian organizations of the West of neglecting to fulfill their duty in other cases.

The first Christians asked themselves whether the new Church was only for the Jews, or for the Gentiles, too. The question received the right answer. In another form, the problem has reappeared in the twentieth century. Christianity is not only for the West. Christ does not belong only to America, England, and other democratic countries. When He was crucified, one of His hands was stretched out toward the west, the other toward the east. He wishes to be the King not only of the Jews, but also of the Gentiles, of the Communists, and of the Western world.

Jesus said, "Go into all the world and preach the gospel to every creature" (Mark 16:15).

He gave His blood for all, and all should hear and believe the gospel.

What encourages us to preach the gospel in captive nations is that there those who become Christians are full of love and zeal. I have never met a single lukewarm Russian Christian. Former young Communists and Muslims become exceptional disciples of Christ.

Christ loves these people and wishes to free them, as He loves all sinners and desires to free them from sin. Some Western church leaders replace this, the only correct attitude, with another one: complacency toward the persecutors of Christians. They favor the sinful, thereby helping the persecutors to maintain their power and hindering the salvation of these same enemies, as well as of their victims.

What I Found Upon My Release

When I was reunited with my wife after my release from prison, she asked me what my plans were for the future. I answered, "The ideal that I have before me is the life of a spiritual recluse." My wife answered that she had had the same thought.

I had been a very dynamic type in my youth. But prison, and especially the years of solitary confinement, had transformed me into a meditative, contemplative man. All the storms in the heart had been stilled. I did not mind communism; I did not even notice it. I was in the embraces of the heavenly Bridegroom. I prayed for those who tormented us and loved them with all of my heart.

I had had very little hope of ever being released. From time to time I wondered what I would do in case I were released. I always considered that I would retire somewhere and continue the life of sweet union in the desert with the heavenly Bridegroom.

God is "the Truth." The Bible is the "truth about the Truth." Theology is the "truth about the truth about the Truth." Christian people live in these many truths about the Truth, and, because of them, have not "the Truth." Hungry, beaten, and drugged, we had forgotten theology and the Bible. We had forgotten the "truths about the Truth," therefore we lived in "the Truth." It is written, "The Son of man is coming at an hour when you do not expect Him" (Matthew 24:44). We could not think anymore. In our darkest hours of torture, the Son of Man came to us, making the prison walls shine like diamonds and filling the cells with light. Somewhere, far away, were the torturers below us in the sphere of the body. But the spirit rejoiced in the Lord. We would not have given up this joy for that of kingly palaces.

The desire to fight against somebody or something could not have been further from my mind. I did not wish to fight any wars, even just wars. I wished rather to build living temples to Christ. It was with the hope of quiet years of contemplation ahead that I left prison.

But, from the very day of my release, I was faced with aspects of communism more ugly than all the tortures of my imprisonment had been. One after the other I met great preachers and pastors of the different churches, and even bishops, who simply confessed with great sorrow that they were informers for the secret police against their own flocks. I asked them if they were prepared to give up being informers, even at the risk of being imprisoned themselves. All answered "no," and explained that it was not fear for their own persons that restrained them. They told me of new developments in the churches, things that did not exist before my arrest—that to refuse to be an informer could mean the closing of a church.

In every town there was a government representative for the control of "cults," a man of the secret Communist police. He had the right to call any priest or pastor whenever he liked and to ask him who had been in church, who took frequent Communion, who was zealous in religion, who was a soul-winner, what people confessed, and so on. If you did not answer, you were dismissed and another "minister" was put in your place who would say more than you did. Where the government representative had no such replacement (which almost never happened), he simply closed the church. This happens today in China.

Most ministers gave information to the secret police. Some did it reluctantly, trying to hide certain things, whereas others got into the habit and their consciences were hardened. Still others had acquired a passion for it and said more than was demanded of them.

I heard confessions from children of Christian martyrs who had been obliged to give information about the families in which they had been received with kindness. Otherwise, they were threatened with not being able to continue their studies.

I went to the Baptist Congress, which was under the token of the Red Flag, where the Communists had decided who should be the "elected leaders." I knew that at the head of all the official churches were men nominated by the Communist Party. Then I realized that I was seeing an abomination about which Jesus spoke.

There have always been good and bad pastors and preachers. But now, for the first time in Church history, the Central Committee of an avowed atheistic Party, which has as its declared purpose the uprooting of religion, decides who leads the Church. To lead it for what purpose? Surely, to help in the uprooting of religion.

Lenin wrote: "Every religious idea, every idea of God—even flirting with the idea of God—is unutterable vileness of the most dangerous kind, contagion of the most abominable kind. Millions of sins, filthy deeds, acts of violence, and physical contagion are far less dangerous than the subtle, spiritual idea of a God."

The Communist Parties of the Soviet Union were Leninist. To them religion was worse than cancer, tuberculosis, or syphilis. *They* decided who should be the religious leaders. The leaders of the official church cooperated, compromising more or less with them.

I have seen the poisoning of children and youth with atheism, the official churches having not the slightest possibility of counteracting it. In no church in our capital of Bucharest could one find a youth meeting or a Sunday school for children. The children of Christians are brought up in the school of hatred.

And then—seeing all this—I hated communism as I had not hated it under their tortures.

I hated not because of what it had done to me, but because of the wrong it does to the glory of God, to the name of Christ, and to the souls of one billion men under its dominion.

Peasants from all over the country came to see me and told me how the collectivization was being conducted. They were now hungry slaves on their own former fields and vineyards. They had no bread. Their children had no milk, no fruit—and this in a country with natural riches that equal those of Canaan of old.

Brethren confessed to me that Lenin's Communist regime had made thieves and liars of them all. Out of hunger they had to steal from what was originally their own field, but now belonged to the collective. Then they had to lie to cover their theft.

Workers spoke to me about the terror in the factories and about an exploitation of work-power such as the capitalists had never dreamed of. The workers had no right to strike.

Intellectuals had to teach, against their inner convictions, that there is no God.

The whole life and thought of one-third of the world at that time was destroyed or falsified, as is still being done in restricted nations today.

Young girls came to complain that they had been called to the Communist Youth Organization, and were reproved and threatened because they kissed a boy who was a Christian; and the name of another was given to them whom they might kiss!

Everything was desperately false and ugly.

Then I met the fighters of the Underground Church—my comrades of long ago—some of whom have remained uncaught and others who have taken up the fight again after having been released from prison. They called on me to take up the fight with them. I attended their secret meetings at which they sang from hymnbooks written by hand.

I remembered St. Anthony the Great, who had been in the desert for thirty years. He had left the world altogether, passing his whole life in fasting and prayer. But when he heard about the fight between St. Athanasius and Arius about the divinity of Christ, he left the contemplative life and came to Alexandria to help the truth to triumph.

I decided to do what all Christians have to do: to follow the examples of Christ, the apostle Paul, and the great saints, to give up the thought of retiring and to take up the fight. What kind of fight would it be?

Christians in prison have always prayed for their enemies and have given a beautiful witness to them. The desire of our heart was that they should be saved, and we rejoiced as often as it happened. But I hated the evil Communist system and I wished to strengthen the Underground Church, the only force that can overthrow this awful tyranny, by the power of the gospel.

I did not think only about Romania, but also about the entire Communist world. However, I have met much unconcern in the West.

Writers around the world protested when two Communist writers, Siniavski and Daniel, were sentenced to prison by their own comrades. But not even churches protest when Christians are put in prison for their faith.

Who cares about Brother Kuzyck, sentenced because he committed the crime of distributing "poisonous" Christian publications such as Bible portions and the devotional booklets of Torrey? Who knows about Brother Prokofiev, sentenced for having distributed printed sermons? Who knows about Grunvald, a Hebrew Christian sentenced for similar offenses in Russia and from whom the Communists took his little son for life? I know what I felt when I was taken away from my Mihai. And I suffer with Brother Grunvald, Ivanenko, Granny Shevchuk, Taisya Tkachenko, Ekaterina Vekazina, Georgi Vekazin, the couple Pilat in Latvia, and on and on—names of saints and heroes of the faith in the twentieth century! I bow to kiss their chains, as the first Christians kissed the chains of their fellow believers when they were led to be thrown before the wild beasts.

Some Western Church leaders don't care about them. The names of the martyrs are not on their prayer lists. While they were being tortured and sentenced, the Russian Baptist and Orthodox official leaders who had denounced and betrayed them were received with great honor at New Delhi, at Geneva, and at other conferences. There they assured everyone that in Russia there is full religious liberty.

A leader of the World Council of Churches kissed the Bolshevik archbishop Nikodim when he gave this assurance. Then they banqueted together in the imposing name of the World Council of Churches, while the saints in prison ate cabbage with unwashed intestines, just as I had eaten in the name of Jesus Christ.

Things could not remain like this. The Underground Church decided that I should leave the country if the possibility were given, and inform Christians in the West about what is happening.

I have decided to denounce communism, though I love the Communists. I don't find it to be right to preach the gospel without denouncing communism.

Some tell me "Preach the pure gospel!" This reminds me that the Communist secret police also told me to preach Christ, but not to mention communism. Is it really so, that those who are for what is called "a pure gospel" are inspired by the same spirit as those of the Communist secret police?

I don't know what this so-called pure gospel is. Was the preaching of John the Baptist pure? He did not say only, "Repent, for the kingdom of heaven is at hand!" (Matthew 3:2). He also "rebuked [Herod] ... for all the evils which Herod had done" (Luke 3:19). He was beheaded because he didn't confine himself to abstract teaching. Jesus did not preach only the "pure" Sermon on the Mount, but also what some actual church leaders would have called a negative sermon: "Woe to you, scribes and Pharisees, hypocrites! ... Serpents, brood of vipers!" (Matthew 23:27,33). It is for such "impure" preaching that He was crucified. The Pharisees would not have bothered about the Sermon on the Mount.

Sin must be called by its name. Communism is one of the most dangerous sins in the world today. Every gospel that does not denounce it is not the pure gospel. The Underground Church denounces it, risking liberty and life. The less have we to be silent in the West.

I have decided to denounce communism, not in the sense in which those who are usually called "anti-Communists" do it. Hitler was an anti-Communist and was nonetheless a tyrant. We hate the sin and love the sinner.

Why I Suffer in the West

I suffer in the West more than I did in Communist lands.

My suffering consists first of all in the longing after the unspeakable beauties of the Underground Church, the Church that fulfills the old Latin saying, *Nudisnudum Christi sequi* (naked, follow the naked Christ).

In captive nations, the Son of Man and those who are His have nowhere to lay their heads. Many Christians there don't build houses for themselves. To what good? They will be confiscated at their first arrest. Just the fact that you have a new house can be a greater motive for you to be imprisoned, because the others wish to take your house. There you don't bury your father, neither do you say farewell to your family before following Christ. Who is your mother, your brother, your sister? You are, in this respect, like Jesus. Mother and brother are for you only those who fulfill the will of God. As for the natural ties, can they count anymore when it is a frequent occurrence that the bride denounces the bridegroom, children their parents, wives their husbands? It is more and more only the spiritual connection that remains.

The Underground Church is a poor and suffering church, but it has few lukewarm members.

A religious service in the Underground Church is like one nineteen hundred years ago in the Early Church. The preacher knows no elaborate theology. He knows no homiletic, as Peter did not know it. Every professor of theology would have given Peter a poor grade for his sermon on the day of Pentecost. The Bible verses are not well known in many countries, because Bibles are not permitted. Besides, the preacher has most likely been in prison for years without a Bible. When they express their faith in a Father, it means much because there is a drama behind this assertion. In prison they have daily asked this almighty Father for bread and have received instead cabbage with unmentionable filth. Nevertheless, they believe God to be the loving Father. They are like Job who said that he would believe in God even if He would slay him. They are like Jesus who called God "Father," even when He was seemingly forsaken on the cross.

Whoever has known the spiritual beauty of the Underground Church cannot be satisfied anymore with the emptiness of some Western churches.

I suffer in the West more than I suffered in a Communist jail because now I see with my own eyes Western civilization dying.

Oswald Spengler wrote in *Decline of the West:*

> You are dying. I see in you all the characteristic stigma of decay. I can prove that your great wealth and your great poverty, your capitalism and your socialism, your wars and your revolutions, your atheism and your pessimism and your cynicism,

your immorality, your broken-down marriages, your birth-control, that is bleeding you from the bottom and killing you off at the top in your brains—can prove to you that there are characteristic marks of the dying ages of ancient states—Alexandria and Greece and neurotic Rome.

This was written in 1926. Since then, democracy and civilization have died already in half of Europe and even as far as Cuba. Much of the West sleeps.

But there is one force that does not sleep. Whereas in the East, Communists are disappointed and have lost their illusions, in the West a "humanistic communism" has remained virulent. The Western humanists/Communists simply do not believe all the bad reports about the cruelties, the misery, and the persecution in Communist countries. They spread their faith with tireless zeal everywhere, in the lounges of the upper classes, in the clubs of intellectuals, in colleges, in the slums, and in the churches. We Christians are often half-heartedly on the side of the whole truth. They are wholeheartedly on the side of the lie.

Theologians of the West discuss trifles in the meantime. It reminds me that, while the troops of Mahomet II surrounded Constantinople in 1493 and it had to be decided whether the Balkans would be under Christian or Muslim dominion for centuries, a local church council in the besieged city discussed the following problems: What color were the eyes of the virgin Mary? What gender do the angels have? If a fly falls into sanctified water, is the fly sanctified or the water defiled? This may be only a legend concerning those times, but peruse Church periodicals of today and you will find that questions just like these are discussed. The menace of the persecutors and the sufferings of the Underground Church are scarcely ever mentioned.

There are endless discussions about theological matters, about rituals, about nonessentials.

At a party in a lounge, someone asked: "If you were on a ship that sank and you could escape to an isolated island, having the chance to take with you only one book from the ship's library, which one would you choose?" One answered, "The Bible," another, "Shakespeare." But a writer had the correct answer: "I would choose a book that could teach me how to make a boat and to arrive on the shore. There I would be free to read whatever I wished."

To keep liberty for all denominations and all theologies, and to regain it where it has been lost due to widespread religious persecution, is more important than to insist upon one certain theological opinion.

"The truth shall make you free," said Jesus (John 8:32). But, the same freedom, only freedom, can give the truth. And, instead of quarreling about nonessentials, we should unite in this fight for freedom against the tyrannies in this world.

I suffer also by sharing the increasing suffering of the Church in captive nations. Having passed through these sufferings, I can visualize them.

In June 1966, the Soviet newspapers *Izvestia* and *Dervenskais Jizn* accused the Russian Baptists of teaching their members to kill children to atone for sins. It is the old accusation of ritual murder that used to be raised against the Jews.

But I know what this means. I was in a prison in Cluj in 1959 with a prisoner, Lazarovici, accused of having killed a girl. He was only thirty years old, but his hair had turned white overnight under the tortures. He looked like an old man. His fingernails had been torn out to make him confess to the crime, which he had not committed. After a year of torture, his innocence was established and he was released, but freedom meant nothing to him any longer. He was a broken man forever.

Others read a newspaper article and laughed about the stupid accusations that the Soviet Press made against the Baptists during the Communist era. I know what they mean for the accused.

It is horrible to be in the West and to have such images constantly before your eyes.

What happened to the Archbishop Yermogen of Kaluga (U.S.S.R.) and the other seven bishops who protested against the extremes of cooperation with the Soviet regime as practiced by the patriarch Alexei and the Archbishop Nikodim, who were tools in the hands of the Communists? If I had not seen the bishops who protested in Romania dying near me in prison, I would not be so concerned about these godly bishops.

The ministers Nikolai Eshliman and Gleb Yakunin were disciplined by the patriarch because they asked for religious freedom for the church. The West knows this much. But I was in prison with Father Ioan of Vladimireshti, Romania, to whom the same thing happened. On the surface there was only an ecclesiastical "disciplining." But our official church leaders, like most official church leaders of the Communist countries, worked hand-in-hand with the secret police. Those disciplined by them were also put under the more efficient "discipline"—tortures, beatings, and drugging—of prisoners.

I tremble because of the sufferings of those persecuted in different lands. I tremble thinking about the eternal destiny of their torturers. I tremble for Western Christians who don't help their persecuted brethren.

In the depth of my heart, I would like to keep the beauty of my own vineyard and not be involved in such a huge fight. I would like so much to be somewhere in quietness and rest. But it is not possible. When the Communists invaded Tibet, they put an end to those who were interested only in completely spiritual matters. In our country they put an end to all who removed themselves from reality. Churches and monasteries were dissolved, keeping only as much as was necessary to dupe foreigners. The quietness and rest for which I long would be an escape from reality and dangerous for my soul.

I have led this fight although it was very dangerous for me personally. They kidnapped me from the street in 1948 and put me in jail under a false name. Anna Pauker, our Secretary of State at that time, said to the Swedish ambassador, Sir Patrick von Reuterswaerde, "Oh, Wurmbrand is now taking walks on the streets of Copenhagen." The Swedish minister had in his pocket my letter that I had succeeded in smuggling out of prison; he knew that he had been told a lie. Such a thing can happen again. If I am killed, the killer will have been appointed by the Communists. No one else has any motive to kill me. If you hear rumors about my moral depravity, theft, homosexuality, adultery, political unreliableness, lying, or anything else, it will be the fulfilling of the threat of the secret police: "We will destroy you morally."

A very well-informed source told me that the Romanian Communists decided to kill me after the testimony I gave to the U.S. Senate in the late 1960s. But I cannot remain silent. And your duty is to examine quietly what I say. Even if you think that, after all I have passed through, I suffer from a persecution complex, you must ask yourself what this dreadful power of communism is that makes its citizens suffer from such complexes. What power is it that made men from Communist East Germany take a child in a bulldozer and pass through barbed wire at the risk of being shot with their whole family?

The West sleeps and must be awakened to see the plight of captive nations.

Men who suffer often seek a scapegoat, someone on whom to place the guilt. To find such a one eases the burden much. I cannot do it.

I cannot put the guilt on some of the Church leaders of the West who compromise with the haters of Christians. The evil comes not from them. These leaders are themselves the victims of a much older evil. They did not create the mess in the Church; they found it.

Since being in the West, I have visited many theological seminaries. There I heard lectures about the history of bells and the history of liturgical songs, about canonical laws long since disused or about a church discipline that no longer exists. I have heard that some students of theology learn that the biblical story of creation is not true, nor that of Adam, nor the flood, nor the miracles of Moses. Some are taught that the prophecies were written after their fulfillment; that the virgin birth is a myth; likewise the resurrection of Jesus, that His bones have remained somewhere in a grave; that the Epistles are not genuine; and that Revelation is the book of a madman. Otherwise, the Bible is a holy book! (This leaves a holy book in which there are allegedly more lies than in Chinese Communist newspapers.)

That is what some present Western Church leaders learned when they were in seminaries. That is the atmosphere in which they live. Why should they be faithful to a Master about whom such strange things are said? Why should Church leaders be faithful to a Church in which it can be freely taught that God is dead?

Some leaders of denominations are not of the Bride of Christ. They are leaders in a Church in which many have long since betrayed the Master. When they meet someone of the Underground Church, a martyr, they look at him strangely.

We cannot always judge man for only one part of his attitude. If we did so, we would be like the Pharisees in whose eyes Jesus was seen as bad, because He did not respect their rules about the Sabbath. They closed their eyes entirely to what would have been lovable in Jesus, even in their sight.

The same Church leaders who have a wrong attitude toward communism may be right in many other things and may be personally sincere. And even in what they are wrong, they may change.

I was once with an Orthodox bishop in Romania. He was a man of the Communists, denouncing his own sheep. I took his hand between mine and told him the parable of the prodigal son. It was on an evening in his garden. I said, "See with what love God receives a sinner who returns. He receives gladly even a bishop if he repents." I sang him Christian songs. This man was converted.

I was in prison in the same cell with an Orthodox priest who, in the hope of being released, wrote atheistic lectures. I spoke to him and he tore to pieces what he had written, thus risking never to be released.

I cannot make a scapegoat of anyone to ease the burden I have upon my heart.

I have another pain. Even very close friends misunderstand me. Some accuse me of bitterness and resentment against the Communists, which I know not to be true.

The Mosaic writer Claude Montefiore said that Jesus' attitude toward scribes and Pharisees, His public denunciation of them, is contrary to His command to love our enemies and bless those who curse us. And Dr. W. R. Matthews, retired Dean of St. Paul's in London, concluded that this is an incoherence and inconsistency in Jesus. He gives the excuse that Jesus was not an intellectual!

Montefiore's impression of Jesus was wrong. Jesus loved the Pharisees, although He denounced them publicly. And I love the Communists, as well as their tools in the Church, although I denounce them.

Constantly I am told, "Forget the Communists! Work only in spiritual things!"

I met with a Christian who had suffered under the Nazis. He told me that he is entirely on my side as long as I witness for Christ, but I should not say one word against communism. I asked him if Christians who fought against Nazism in Germany were wrong and if they should have been confined to speaking only from the Bible, without saying a word against the tyrant Hitler. The reply was, "But Hitler killed six million Jews! One *had* to speak against him." I replied, "communism has killed thirty million Russians and millions of Chinese and others. And they have killed Jews, too. Must we protest only when Jews are killed, and not when Russians or Chinese are killed?" The answer was, "This is quite another thing." I received no explanation.

The police beat me both during Hitler's reign and during Communist times, and I could not see any difference. Both were very painful.

Christianity has to fight against many aspects of sin, not only against communism. We are not obsessed with just this one problem. But communism is a tremendous foe of Christianity and most dangerous. Against it, we must unite.

May I say it again! The highest goal of man is to become Christ-like. To prevent this is the main aim of Communists. They are primarily anti-religious. They believe that after death man becomes salt and minerals, nothing else. They desire the whole life to be lived on the level of matter.

They know only the masses. Their word is that of the demon in the New Testament when asked what his name was: "We are legion." Individual personality—one of the great gifts of God to mankind—must be crushed. They imprisoned a man because they found him with a book by Alfred Adler, *Individual Psychology*. The officers of the secret police shouted, "Ah, individual—always individual! Why not collective?"

Jesus wishes us to be personalities. Therefore there is no possibility of compromise between communism and us. The Communists know it. In their magazine *Nauka i Religia* (Science and Religion), they have written, "Religion is incompatible with communism. It is hostile to it ... The content of the program of the Communist Party is a death blow to religion ... It is a program for the creation of an atheistic society in which people will be rid forever of the religious bondage."

Can Christianity coexist with communism? Here the Communists answer this question: "The Communist Party is a death blow to religion!"

Chapter 5

The Invincible, Widespread Underground Church

The Underground Church works under very difficult conditions. Atheism is the state religion in all the Communist countries. They give relative freedom for the elderly to believe, but children and youth must not believe. Everything in these countries and other kinds of captive nations—radio, television, cinema, theater, press, and publishing houses—has the aim of stamping out belief in Jesus Christ.

The Underground Church has very little means of opposing the huge forces of the totalitarian state. The underground ministers in Russia had no theological training. There are Chinese pastors today who have never read the entire Bible.

I will tell you how numerous pastors have been ordained. We met a young Russian who was a secret minister. I asked him who ordained him. He answered, "We had no real bishop to ordain us. The official bishop would not ordain anyone who is not approved by the Communist Party. So ten of us young Christians went to the tomb of a bishop who died as a martyr. Two of us put our hands on his gravestone and the others formed a circle around us. We asked the Holy Spirit to ordain us. We are sure that we were ordained by the pierced hands of Jesus." For me, this young man's ordination is valid before God!

Men with such ordination, who have never had any theological training and who very often know little of the Bible (such as evangelists in Bangladesh), carry on the work of Christ.

It is like the Church in the first centuries. What seminaries did those who turned the world upside-down for Christ attend? Did they all know how to read? And from where did they receive Bibles? God spoke to them.

We of the Underground Church have no cathedrals. But is any cathedral more beautiful than the sky of heaven to which we looked when we gathered secretly in forests? The chirping of birds took the place of the organ. The fragrance of flowers was our incense. And the shabby suit of a martyr recently freed from prison was much more impressive than priestly robes. We had the moon and stars as candles. The angels were our acolytes who lit them.

I can never describe the beauty of this Church! Often, after a secret service, Christians were caught and sent to prison. There, Christians wear chains with the gladness with which a bride wears a precious jewel received from her beloved. The waters in prison are still. They receive His kiss and His embraces, and would not change places with kings. I have found truly joyful Christians only in the Bible, in the Underground Church, and in prison.

The Underground Church is oppressed, but it also has many friends—even among the secret police; even among members of the government. Sometimes these secret believers protect the Underground Church.

Under the former Soviet Empire, Russian newspapers complained of the growing numbers of "outward nonbelievers." These, the Russian press explained, are countless men and women who work in the very echelons of Communist power—in government offices, in propaganda departments, and elsewhere—who outwardly are Communists, but inwardly are secret believers and members of the Underground Church.

The Communist press told the story of a young woman who worked in the Communist propaganda department. After work, they said, she and her husband would gather a group of young people from other apartments in their building for secret Bible studies and prayer meetings. This is still happening throughout the world. Tens of thousands of such "outward nonbelievers" exist. They feel it wiser not to attend the show-churches where they will be watched and hear only a watered-down gospel. Instead, they stay in their positions of authority and responsibility from which they can quietly and effectively witness for Christ.

The faithful Underground Church has thousands of members in such places. They have secret meetings in basements, attics, apartments, and fields.

In formerly Communist Russia, no one remembered anymore the arguments for or against child or adult baptism, for or against papal infallibility. They were not pre- or post-millennialists. They could not interpret prophecies and didn't quarrel about them, but I wondered very often how well they could prove to atheists the existence of God.

Their answers to atheists were simple: "If you were invited to a feast with all kinds of good meats, would you believe that there has been no one to cook them? But nature is a banquet prepared for us! You have tomatoes and peaches and apples and milk and honey. Who has prepared all these things for mankind? Nature is blind. If you believe in no God, how can you explain that blind nature succeeded in preparing just the things that we need in such plenitude and variety?"

They prove that eternal life exists. I heard one pleading with an atheist: "Suppose that we could speak with an embryo in his mother's womb and that you would tell him that the embryonic life is only a short one after which follows a real, long life. What would the embryo answer? He would say just what you atheists answer to us, when we speak to you about paradise and hell. He would say that the life in the mother's womb is the only one and that everything else is religious foolishness. But if the embryo could think, he would say to himself, 'Here arms grow on me. I do not need them. I cannot even stretch them. Why do they grow? Perhaps they grow for a future stage of my existence, in which I will have to work with them. Legs grow, but I have to keep them bent toward my chest. Why do they grow? Probably life in a large world follows, where I will have to walk. Eyes grow, although I am surrounded by perfect darkness and don't need them. Why do I have eyes? Probably a world with light and colors will follow.'

"So, if the embryo would reflect on his own development, he would know about a life outside of his mother's womb, without having seen it. It is the same with us. As long as we are young, we have vigor, but no mind to use it properly. When, with the years, we have grown in knowledge and wisdom, the hearse waits to take us to the grave. Why was it necessary to grow in a knowledge and wisdom that we can use no more? Why do arms, legs, and eyes grow on an embryo? *It is for what follows.* So it is with us here. We grow here in experience, knowledge, and wisdom for what follows. We are prepared to serve on a higher level that follows death."

About Jesus, the Communists printed that He never existed. The workers of the Underground Church answered this easily: "What newspaper have you in your pocket? Is it the *Pravda* of today or yesterday? Let me have a look. Aha! January 4, 1964. The year 1964 counted from when? You say Jesus never existed, yet you count the years from His birth. Time existed before Him. But when He came, it seemed to mankind that everything which had been before had been vain and that the real time began only now. Your Communist newspaper itself is a proof that Jesus is not fiction."

Pastors in the West usually assume that those whom they have in church are really convinced about the main truths of Christianity, which they are not. You rarely hear a sermon proving the truth of our faith. But behind the Iron Curtain, men who have never learned to do it gave their converts a very serious foundation.

There is no clear dividing line by which you could say where the Underground Church, which is the main stronghold of

Christianity, ends and the official Church begins. They are inter-woven. Some pastors of the show-churches in captive nations carry on a secret parallel ministry going far beyond the limitations imposed on them by their governments.

The official Church, the church of collaborators with the Communists, has a long history. It began immediately after the Russian Socialist Revolution with the "Living Church," headed by a bishop named Sergius. One of his collaborators declared that "Marxism is the gospel written with atheist letters." What nice theology.

We have had many like Sergius in every country.

In Hungary, among the Catholics, it was Father Balogh. He and some Protestant ministers helped the Communists take com-plete control of the state.

In Romania, the Communists came to power with the help of an Orthodox priest named Burducea, a former Fascist, who had to make up to the Reds for his past sins by becoming even more "Red" than his bosses. This priest stood near Vishinski, the Soviet Secretary of State, and smiled in an approving manner when the latter declared at the installation of the new Communist govern-ment: "This government will build an earthly paradise and you will no longer need a heavenly one."

As for those like Nikolai of Russia, it is on record that they are informers for the government. Major Deriabin, a defector from the Russian secret police, testified that Nikolai was their agent.

This was the situation in nearly all denominations. The leader-ship of the Romanian Baptists was imposed by force, denouncing the real Christians. In Russia the leadership of the Baptists did the same. The president of the Romanian Adventists, Tachici, told me that he had been an informer of the Communist secret police from the first day they came to power.

Rather than close every church—though they have closed many thousands—the Communists shrewdly decided to permit a few "token" official churches to remain open and use them as windows through which to observe, control, and eventually destroy Christians and Christianity. They decided that it would be better to let the structure of the Church remain and turn it into a Communist tool to control Christians and to deceive visitors coming to their lands. This situation exists in the official Chinese TSPM church as we move into the next century. This "only legal" church in China represents less than twenty percent of China's Christians.

In Romania, I was offered such a church on the condition that I, as pastor, would report on my members to the secret police. It seems that Westerners, accustomed to things "black and white"—all one way or all another—cannot understand this. But the Underground Church will never accept token, controlled churches as a substitute for meaningful, effective evangelism "to every creature"—including youth.

But in the official churches there is a real spiritual life, despite many treacherous leaders. (I have the impression that in many churches of the West the situation is similar. The congregations are faithful sometimes not because of, but in spite of, their top leaders.)

In Russia, the Orthodox liturgy remained unchanged, and it fed the hearts of the members of this church, even if the sermons flattered the Communists. The Lutherans, Presbyterians, and other Protestants sang the same old hymns. And then, even the sermons of the informers had to contain something of Scripture. People in China today are converted under the influence of men whom they know to be traitors. They know that they will tell the secret police about their conversions. They must hide their faith from the very one who gave them this faith by his corrupted sermon. This is the great miracle of God cited in Leviticus 11:37 in symbolic language: "And if a part of any such carcass [which is, according to the Mosaic law, defiled] falls on any planting seed which is to be sown, it remains clean."

Fairness obliges us to say that not all the official Church leaders, not even all the official top leaders, are men of the Communists.

Members of the Underground Church are also very prominent in the official churches, except for some who have to keep themselves hidden. And they see to it that Christianity is not wishy-washy, but a fighting faith. When the secret police came to close down the monastery of Vladimireshti in Romania and others in many places in Russia, they had a hard time. Some Communists have paid with their lives for the crime of trying to forbid religion.

But the official churches are becoming fewer and fewer. I wonder if, in the whole of the Soviet Union, there were five or six thousand churches under communism. (The United States, with the same population, had some three hundred thousand decades ago.) And these "churches" were most often only tiny rooms—not a "church" as we picture it. Foreign visitors would see a crowded church in Moscow—which was the only Protestant church in the city—and remark what freedom there is. "Even the churches are overflowing!" they would joyously report. They did not see the tragedy of one Protestant church for seven million souls! And not even the one-room churches were within traveling distance of eighty percent of the people of the Soviet Union. These multitudes were either forgotten or reached with underground methods of evangelism. There was no other choice.

The more communism dominates in a country, the more the Church will have to be underground.

In place of closed official churches come the meetings of the anti-religious organizations.

How the Underground Church "Feeds" on Atheistic Literature

The Underground Church knows how to use atheistic literature, too, feeding upon it just as Elijah was fed by ravens. The atheists put much skill and zeal into ridiculing and criticizing Bible verses.

They published books called *The Comical Bible* and *The Bible for Believers and Unbelievers*. They tried to show how stupid Scripture is and, to do so, quoted many Bible verses. How we rejoiced over it! The book was printed in millions of copies and was full of Bible verses, which were unspeakably beautiful even when the Communists ridiculed them. The criticism itself was so stupid that no one took it seriously. In the past, "heretics" burned by the

Inquisition were taken to the stake in a procession, dressed in all kinds of ridiculous clothes with hell-flames and devils painted on them. And what saints were these heretics! In a similar way, Bible verses remain true, even if the Devil quotes them.

The Communist publishing house was very glad to receive thousands of letters asking for reprints of atheist books that quoted Bible verses to mock them. They did not know that these letters came from the Underground Church, which had no other opportunity of receiving the Scriptures.

We also knew well how to use the atheistic meetings.

A professor of communism demonstrated at a meeting that Jesus was nothing but a magician. The professor had before him a pitcher of water. He put a powder in it and it became red. "This is the whole miracle," he explained. "Jesus had hidden in his sleeves a powder like this, and then pretended to have changed water into wine in a wonderful manner. But I can do even better than Jesus; I can change the wine into water again." And he put another powder in the liquid. It became clear. Then another powder and it was red again.

A Christian stood up and said, "You have amazed us, comrade professor, by what you are able to do. We would ask only one thing more of you—drink a bottle of your wine!" The professor said, "This I cannot do. The powder was a poison." The Christian replied, "This is the whole difference between you and Jesus. He, with His wine, has given us joy for two thousand years, whereas you poison us with your wine." The Christian went to prison. But news of the incident spread very far and strengthened many of the faith.

We are weak little Davids. But we are stronger than the Goliath of atheism, because God is on our side. The truth belongs to us.

On one occasion a Communist was giving a lecture on atheism. All factory workers were required to attend; among these workers were many Christians. They sat quietly hearing all the arguments against God and about the stupidity of believing in Christ. The lecturer attempted to prove that there is no spiritual world, no God, no Christ, no hereafter; man is only matter with no soul. He said over and over that only matter exists.

A Christian stood up and asked to speak. Permission was given. The Christian picked up his folding chair and threw it down. He paused, looking at it. He then walked up and slapped the Communist lecturer in the face. The lecturer became very angry. His face flushed red with indignation. He shouted obscenities and called for fellow Communists to arrest the Christian. He demanded, "How dare you slap me? What is the reason?"

The Christian replied, "You have just proved yourself a liar. You said everything is matter ... nothing else. I picked up a chair and threw it down. It is truly matter. The chair did not become angry. It is only matter. When I slapped you, you did not react like the chair. You reacted differently. Matter does not get mad or angry, but *you* did. Therefore, comrade professor, you are wrong. Man is more than matter. We are spiritual beings!"

In countless ways such as this, ordinary Christians of the Underground Church disproved elaborate atheistic arguments.

In prison, the political officer asked me harshly, "How long will you continue to keep your stupid religion?" I said to him, "I have seen innumerable atheists regretting on their deathbeds that they have been godless; they called on Christ. Can you imagine that a Christian could regret, when death is near, that he has been a Christian and call on Marx or Lenin to rescue him from his faith?"

The officer laughed, "A clever answer." I continued, "When an engineer has built a bridge, the fact that a cat can pass over the bridge is no proof that the bridge is good. A train must pass over it to prove its strength. The fact that you can be an atheist when everything goes well does not prove the truth of atheism. It does not hold up in moments of great crisis." I used Lenin's books to prove to him that, even after becoming prime minister of the Soviet Union, Lenin himself prayed when things went wrong.

We were quiet and could quietly await the development of events. It was the Communists who were unquiet and launched new anti-religious campaigns. By this they proved what St. Augustine said, "Uneasy is the heart until it rests in Thee."

Why Even Communists Can Be Won

The Underground Church, if helped by Christians in the free world, will win the hearts of the Communists and will change the face of the world. It *will* win them, because it is unnatural to be a Communist. Even a dog wishes to have his own bone. The hearts of Communists rebel against the role they must play and the absurdities they are forced to believe.

Individual Communists asserted that "matter is everything"— that we are a handful of chemicals organized in a certain fashion and that after death we will again be salt and minerals. It was therefore enough to ask them, "How is it that Communists in so many countries have given their lives for their belief? Does a 'handful of chemicals' have beliefs? Can 'minerals' sacrifice themselves for the good of others?" To this they have no answer.

And then there is the issue of brutality. Men were not created as brutes and cannot bear to be brutes for long. We have seen it in the collapse of Nazi rulers, some of whom committed suicide, while some repented and confessed their crimes.

The enormous amount of drunkenness in Communist countries exposes the longing for a more meaningful life, which communism cannot give. The average Russian is a deep, big-hearted, generous person. communism is shallow and superficial. He seeks the deep life and, finding it nowhere else, he seeks it in alcohol. He expresses in alcoholism his horror about the brutal and deceitful life he must live. For a few moments alcohol sets him free, as truth would set him free forever if he could know it.

In Bucharest, during the Russian occupation (1947–1989), I once felt an irresistible impulse to enter a tavern. I called my wife to go with me. Upon entering, we saw a Russian captain with a gun in his hand threatening everyone and asking for more to drink. He had been refused because he was already very drunk. People were in a panic. I went to the owner—who knew me—and asked him to give liquor to the captain, promising that I would sit with him and see that he kept quiet. One bottle of wine after another was given to us. On the table were three glasses. The captain always politely filled all three ... and drank all three. My wife and I did not drink. Although he was very drunk, his mind was working. He was used to alcohol. I spoke to him about Christ and he listened with unexpected attention.

When I finished, he said, "Now that you have told me who you are, I will tell you who I am. I am an Orthodox priest who was among the first to deny my faith when the great persecution under Stalin began. I went from village to village to give lectures saying that there is no God and that as a priest I had been a deceiver. 'I am a deceiver and so are all the other ministers,' I told them. I was very much appreciated for my zeal, so I became an officer of the secret police. My punishment from God was that with this hand I had to kill Christians, after having tortured them. And now I drink and drink to forget what I have done. But it does not work."

Many Communists commit suicide. So did their greatest poets, Essenin and Maiakovski. So did their great writer Fadeev. He had just finished his novel called *Happiness* in which he had explained that happiness consists in working tirelessly for communism. He was so happy about it that he shot himself after having finished the novel. It was too difficult for his soul to bear such a great lie. Joffe, Tomkin—great Communist leaders and fighters for communism in Czarist times—likewise could not bear to see how communism looks in reality. They also ended in suicide.

Communists are unhappy. So are even their great dictators. How unhappy Stalin was! After having killed nearly all of his old comrades, he was constantly in fear of being poisoned or killed himself. He had eight bedrooms that could be locked up like safes in a bank. No one ever knew in which of these bedrooms he slept on any given night. He never ate unless the cook tasted the food in his presence. Communism makes no one happy, not even its dictators. They need Christ.

By converting those who persecute Christians, we would free not only their victims, but the persecutors themselves.

The Underground Church represents the deepest need of enslaved peoples in captive nations. Help her!

The distinctive feature of the Underground Church is its earnestness in faith.

A minister who disguises himself under the name of "George" tells in his book about God's Underground the following incident:

A Russian Army captain came to a minister in Hungary and asked to see him alone. The young captain was very brash, and very conscious of his role as a conqueror. When he had been led to a small conference room and the door was closed, he nodded toward the cross that hung on the wall.

"You know that thing is a lie," he said to the minister. "It's just a piece of trickery you ministers use to delude the poor people to make it easier for the rich to keep them ignorant. Come now, we are alone. Admit to me that you never really believed that Jesus Christ was the Son of God!"

The minister smiled. "But, my poor young man, of course I believe it. It is true."

"I won't have you play these tricks on me!" cried the captain. "This is serious. Don't laugh at me!"

He drew out his revolver and held it close to the body of the minister.

"Unless you admit to me that it is a lie, I'll fire!"

"I cannot admit that, for it is not true. Our Lord is really and truly the Son of God," said the minister.

The captain flung his revolver on the floor and embraced the man of God. Tears sprang to his eyes.

"It is true!" he cried. "*It is true.* I believe so, too, but I could not be sure men would die for this belief until I found it out for myself. Oh, thank you! You have strengthened my faith. Now I too can die for Christ. You have shown me how."

I have known other such cases. When the Russians occupied Romania, two armed Russian soldiers entered a church with their guns in their hands. They said, "We don't believe in your faith. Those who do not abandon it immediately will be shot at once! Those who abandon your faith move to the right!" Some moved to the right, who were then ordered to leave the church and go home. They fled for their lives. When the Russians were alone with the remaining Christians, they embraced them and confessed, "We, too, are Christians, but we wished to have fellowship only with those who consider the truth worth dying for."

Such men fought for the gospel and still fight today in the Communist nations of Southeast Asia. And they fight not only for the gospel. They are also the fighters for liberty.

In the homes of many Western Christians, hours are sometimes spent listening to worldly music. In our homes loud music can also be heard, but it is only to cover the talk about the gospel and the underground work so that neighbors may not overhear it and inform the secret police.

How underground Christians rejoice on those rare occasions when they meet a serious Christian from the West!

The one who writes these lines is only an insignificant man. But I am the voice of those who are voiceless; of those who are muzzled and never represented in the West. In their name I ask great seriousness in faith and in handling the problems of Christianity. In their name I ask your prayers and practical help for the faithful, suffering Underground Church in Communist lands and other captive nations today.

We *shall* win the Communists. First, because God is on our side. Second, because our message corresponds to the deepest needs of the heart.

Communists who had been in prison under the Nazis confessed to me that they prayed in difficult hours. I have even seen Communist officers die with the words "Jesus, Jesus," on their lips.

We shall win because all the cultural inheritance of our people is on our side. The Russians can forbid all the writings of modern Christians. But there are the books of Tolstoy and Dostoyevski, and people find the light of Christ there. So it is with Goethe in

Eastern Germany, Sienkiewicz in Poland, and others. The greatest Romanian writer was Sadoveanu. The Communists have published his book *The Lives of Saints* under the title *The Legend of Saints*. But even under this title the example of the lives of saints inspires.

They cannot exclude reproductions of Raphael, Michelangelo, and Leonardo da Vinci from the history of the arts. These pictures speak of Christ.

When I talk with a Communist about Christ, the deepest spiritual need in his heart is my ally—my helper. The greatest difficulty for him is not to answer my arguments. His great difficulty is to quiet the voice of his own conscience, which is on my side.

I have personally known professors of Marxism who, before delivering an atheistic lecture, prayed to God that He might help them in this! I have known of Communists going to a secret meeting far away. When they were discovered, they denied that they had been in an underground meeting. Then they wept, regretting that they had not had the courage to stand for the faith that compelled them to attend. They are men, too.

Once the individual has arrived at faith—even a very primitive faith—this faith develops and grows. We are sure that it will conquer because we of the Underground Church have seen it conquer again and again.

Christ loves the Communists and other "enemies of the faith." They can and must be won for Christ. Whoever wishes to satisfy the longing of the heart of Jesus for the salvation of the souls of all mankind should sustain the Underground Church in her work. Jesus said, "Teach all nations." He never said that we need governmental permission to evangelize. Faithfulness to God and the Great Commission compels us to reach beyond borders to people in restricted nations.

We can reach them by working with the Underground Church already there!

Components of the Underground Church

Three groups compose the Underground Church. The first group is the thousands upon thousands of former pastors and ministers who have been removed from their churches and from their flocks because they would not compromise the gospel. Many such pastors and ministers have been imprisoned for years and tortured for their faith. They have been released—and have promptly resumed their ministry—secretly and effectively ministering in the Underground Church. Though the Communists and other types of governments closed their churches or replaced them with more "reliable" ministers, these pastors continue their ministry more effectively than ever by working secretly in underground meetings in barns, attics, basements, and hayfields at night—or anywhere believers gather secretly. These men are "living martyrs" who will not cease their ministry and who risk more torture and re-arrest.

The second part of the Underground Church is the vast army of dedicated lay people. One out of every five people in the world live in Communist China, where thousands of lay Christians evangelize without "permission." Persecution has always produced a better Christian—a witnessing Christian, a soul-winning Christian. Communist persecution has backfired and produced serious, dedicated Christians such as are rarely seen in free lands. These people cannot understand how anyone can be a Christian and not want to win every soul they meet.

The *Red Star* (the Russian Army newspaper) attacked the Russian Christians, saying, "The worshippers of Christ like to get their greedy claws on everyone." But their shining Christian lives won the love and respect of their fellow villagers and neighbors. In any village or town, the Christians were the most liked, beloved residents. When a mother was too ill to care for her children, it was the Christian mother who came over and looked after them. When a man was too ill to cut his firewood, it was the Christian man who did it for him. They *lived* their Christianity, and when they began to witness for Christ the people listened and believed—because they had seen Christ in their lives. Since no one but a licensed minister can speak in an official church, the millions of fervent, dedicated Christians in every corner of the Communist world win souls, witness, and minister in marketplaces, at the village water pump—everywhere they go. Communist newspapers admitted that Christian butchers slipped gospel tracts in the wrapping paper of the meat they sold. The Communist press admitted that Christians working in places of authority in Communist printing houses slipped back in late at night, started up their presses, and ran off a few thousand pieces of Christian literature—and locked up again before the sun arose. The Communist press also admitted that Christian children in Moscow received Gospels from "some sources" and then copied portions by hand. The children then placed the portions in the pockets of their teachers' overcoats that hung in school closets. The vast body of laymen and laywomen is a very powerful, effective, soul-winning missionary force already in every Communist land.

These millions of dedicated, true, and fervent believers in the lay church have been purified by the very fires of persecution that the Communists hoped would destroy them.

In Communist Cuba, thousands of house churches have sprung up despite government harassment. The ecumenical council of Cuba is mainly composed of Marxist church leaders.

The third vital part of the Underground Church is the large body of faithful pastors in the official, but bridled and silenced "churches." The Underground Church is not something completely separate from the official church. During the reign of communism in Poland, Hungary, and the former Yugoslavia, many of the pastors of the official churches secretly worked in the Underground Church. In some countries there is an interweaving between the two even today. These pastors are not allowed to speak about Christ outside their tiny, one-room churches. They are not allowed to have children's meetings or youth meetings. Non-Christians are afraid to come. The pastors are not allowed to pray for ill church members in their homes. They are fenced in on every side by Communist regulations that make their "churches" all but meaningless.

Very often these pastors, faced with controls that make a mockery of "freedom of religion," courageously risk their liberty by carrying on a parallel secret ministry that goes far beyond the government's limitations. These pastors secretly minister to children and youth. In the Middle East, North Africa, and Asia, they evangelize secretly in Christian homes and basements. They secretly receive and distribute Christian literature to hungry souls. They risk their freedom by secretly ignoring the official limitations and ministering to hungry souls all around them. Seemingly docile and obedient on the surface, they risk their lives to secretly spread the Word of God. Many such men were discovered and arrested in the former Soviet Union and received several years of imprisonment.

More men and women are arrested today. They are the vital parts of the Underground Church in restricted nations.

Former ministers who have been expelled from their churches and persecuted by government officials, the lay church, and official pastors who secretly carry on a much larger and extensive ministry than they are permitted—all these are working in the Underground or "unofficial" Church. And the Underground Church will last until communism and other "isms" are defeated. In some lands, one part is more active than another—but all are there, working for Christ at a great risk.

A man who travels frequently in Communist lands and who is very interested in religious questions came back and wrote that he never met any of the Underground Church.

It is like traveling in Central Africa among uneducated tribes and coming back saying, "I inquired thoroughly. I asked them all if they speak prose. They all told me that they don't." The truth is that they all speak prose not knowing that what they speak is prose.

The Christians of the first decades did not know they were Christians. If you had asked them about their religion, they would have answered you that they were Jews, Israelites, believers in Jesus as Messiah, brethren, saints, children of God. The name "Christian" was given to them by others much later, for the first time in Antioch.

None of the followers of Luther knew he was a Lutheran. Luther protested vigorously against this name.

"Underground Church" is a name given by the Communists, as well as by Western researchers of the religious situation in the East, to a secret organization that formed spontaneously in all Communist nations. The members of the Underground Church don't call their organization by this name. They call themselves Christians, believers, children of God. But they lead an underground work, they meet secretly, they spread the gospel in clandestine meetings, attended sometimes by the very foreigners who claim that they did not see the Underground Church. It is an adequate name given by the adversaries and by those who look lovingly from the outside to this wonderful secret organization.

You can travel years throughout the West never meeting an international spy net, which does not mean that this spy net does not exist. It is not so stupid as to show itself to the curious travelers.

In the next chapter, I will quote some articles printed decades ago by the Soviet press, proving the existence and growing importance of this courageous Underground Church.

Chapter 6

How Christianity Is Defeating Communism

I have told of our own experience in spreading Christ's message secretly in the Soviet army as well as in Communist Romania. I have appealed to you to help preach Christ to the Communists and to the people oppressed by them. Is my challenge "visionary" and "unworkable"? Is it realistic?

Does the Underground Church exist now in Communist Asia and other captive nations? Is underground work still possible there now?

To these questions we can answer with very good news.

The Communists celebrated well over half a century of Communist rule. But their victory was a defeat. Christianity has won—not communism. The Russian press, which our organization researched thoroughly, was full of negative propaganda about the Underground Church. The Russian Underground Church had become so strong that it worked even semi-publicly, frightening the Communists. And now the present leadership of the former Soviet Union confirms the reports of the Communist press.

Remember, the Underground Church around the world today is like an iceberg. It is mostly below the surface, but often a small part operates in the open.

In the following pages I have preserved a short compilation of some of their victorious work in the twentieth century.

The Tip of the Iceberg

On November 7, 1966, in Suhumi (Caucasus), the Underground Church held a great meeting under the open skies. Many believers came from other cities to attend this meeting. After the altar call, forty-seven young people accepted Christ and were baptized on the spot in the Black Sea, just as in biblical times.

After decades of Communist dictatorship, having no Bibles, other Christian books, or seminaries, the ministers of the Underground Church are not trained theologians. But neither was Philip, the deacon. Yet a eunuch, with whom he had spoken for perhaps only an hour, asked him, "'See, here is water. What hinders me from being baptized?' Then Philip said, 'If you believe with all your heart, you may.' ... And both Philip and the eunuch went down into the water, and he baptized him" (Acts 8:36–38).

There is enough water in the Black Sea, so the Underground Church reinstated the practices of the biblical time. Today, although the Communist Party no longer rules in Russia, Christians in several of the former Soviet republics face persecution.

Uchitelskaia Gazeta (The Teacher's Magazine) of August 23, 1966, states that a demonstration was organized in the streets of Rostov-on-Don by Baptists who refused to register their congregation and to obey their so-called "leaders" appointed by the Communists.

This occurred on the first of May. As Jesus performed miracles on the Sabbath days to defy his Pharisaic opponents, the Underground Church sometimes chose Communist celebration days for defying the Communist laws. The first of May is a feast on which the Communists always have their great demonstrations, which everyone is compelled to attend. But on this day, the second big force in Russia—the Underground Church—also appeared on the streets.

Fifteen hundred believers came. What compelled them was the love of God. They knew that they risked their liberty, and that in prison starvation and torture awaited them.

Every believer in Russia knew the "Secret Manifesto" printed by the Evangelical Christians in Barnaul, which describes how sister Hmara, of the village of Kulunda, received the news that her husband had died in prison. She was left a widow with four small children. When she received the corpse of her husband, she could see the prints of manacles on his hands. The hands, fingers, and the bottom of his feet were horribly burned. The lower part of his stomach had knife marks on it. The right foot was swollen. On both feet were signs of beating. The whole body was full of wounds from horrible torture.

Every believer who attended the public demonstration in Rostov-on-Don knew this could be his fate, too. Still they came.

But they also knew that this martyr, who had given his life for God only three months after his conversion, was buried before a great crowd of believers who had placards with these inscriptions:

"For to me, to live is Christ, and to die is gain" (Philippians 1:21).

"Do not fear those who kill the body but cannot kill the soul" (Matthew 10:28).

"I saw under the altar the souls of those who had been slain for the Word of God" (Revelation 6:9).

The example of this martyr inspired those in Rostov-on-Don. They crowded around a little house. People were everywhere— some on nearby roofs, others in the trees, like Zacchaeus. Eighty people were converted, mostly young people. Out of this number, twenty-three were former Komsomols (members of the Communist Youth Organization)!

The Christians crossed the entire city walking toward the river Don, where the new believers were baptized.

Automobiles loaded with Communist police soon arrived. The police surrounded the believers on the bank of the river, wanting to arrest the brethren in charge. (They couldn't arrest all fifteen hundred!) The believers immediately fell to their knees and, in a fervent prayer, asked God to defend His people and permit them to have their service for that day. Then the brothers and sisters—standing shoulder to shoulder—surrounded the brethren leading the service, hoping to prevent the police from arresting them. The situation became very tense.

Uchitelskaia Gazeta reported that the "illegal" Baptist organization in Rostov had an underground printing press. (In Russia, the word "Baptist" included Evangelicals and Pentecostals.) In these underground publications, youth were called to stand for their faith, and Christian parents were asked to do what I also think is a very good thing: "to take their children to attend burials in order to learn not to worry about transitory things." Parents were also encouraged to give a Christian education to their children as an antidote against the atheism with which they were poisoned in Communist schools.

Uchitelskaia Gazeta finished the article by asking, "Why do teachers mix so timidly in the life of families in which children are *idiotized* [by religion]?"

This "Teacher's Magazine" also described what happened at the trial of the underground workers who had baptized secretly: "The youthful believers called as witnesses were defiant and contemptuous of the Communist court. They behaved angrily and fanatically. Young women spectators gazed with admiration at the defendants and with disapproval at the atheistic public."

Members of the Underground Church have risked beatings and imprisonment to appeal for more freedom, in front of the Communist Party headquarters in Russia.

We possess a document that had been smuggled to the West through secret channels. This document is from the "illegal"

Committee of the Evangelical Baptist Churches of the Soviet Union (as opposed to the Communist-controlled "Baptist Union" led by the traitor Karev, who praised the humanity of the Communist mass-killers of Christians and magnified the "liberty" reigning there).

In this secret document, we are told about another heroic public demonstration, this time in Moscow itself.

I translate from this manifesto:

Urgent communication.

Beloved Brethren and Sisters,

Blessings to you and peace from God our Father and our Lord Jesus Christ. We hasten to tell you that the delegates of the churches of Evangelical Baptist Christians, numbering five hundred, who traveled to Moscow on May 16, 1966, for intervention with the central organs of power, went to the building of the Central Committee for the Communist Party of the Union of Socialist Soviet Republics, with the request to be received and heard. We delivered a petition addressed to the general secretary, Brezhnev.

The manifesto further stated that these five hundred men stood the entire day before the building. It was the first public demonstration in Moscow against communism. And it was made by the delegation of the Underground Church. At the end of the day they delivered a second petition addressed to Brezhnev, in which they complained that a certain "comrade" Stroganov refused to transmit their request to Brezhnev and threatened them.

The five hundred delegates remained on the streets throughout the night in spite of rain. Although they were verbally insulted and had mud splashed on them by passing cars, they remained until morning in front of the building of the Communist Party!

On the next day it was proposed that the five hundred brethren should enter a building to meet some minor Communist officials. But "knowing that believers who had visited the authorities were often beaten when they entered a building where there were no witnesses, these believers refused unanimously and continued to wait to be received by Brezhnev."

Then the inevitable happened.

At 1:45 p.m., twenty-eight buses came and the brutal revenge against the believers began. "We formed a ring and, holding each other's hand, we sang the hymn, 'The best days of our life are the days when we can bear a cross.' The men of the secret police began to beat us, the young and old ones. They took men out of the row and beat them on the face and head, then threw them on the asphalt. They dragged some of the brethren to the buses by their hair. When some tried to leave, they were beaten until they lost consciousness. After filling the buses with believers, the police took them to an unknown place. The songs of our brethren and sisters were heard from the secret police buses. All this happened in the sight of a multitude of men."

And now something more beautiful follows. After the five hundred were arrested and surely tortured, Brother G. Vins and another leading brother, named Horev (the real shepherds of Christ's flock), still had the courage to go to the same Central Committee of the Communist Party—just as after the arrest of John the Baptist, Jesus began His public preaching in the same place and with the same words for which John the Baptist suffered: "Repent, for the kingdom of heaven is at hand" (Matthew 4:17).

Vins and Horev asked where the arrested delegation was and demanded their release. These two courageous brethren simply disappeared. Afterward, news was received that they were put in Lefortovskaia prison.

Were these Christians of the Underground Church afraid? No! Others immediately risked their liberty again, publishing the manifesto that we have before us, telling the story of what happened, saying that to them, "For to you it has been granted on behalf of Christ, not only to believe in Him, but also to suffer for His sake" (Philippians 1:29). They exhorted the brethren "that no one should be shaken by these afflictions; for you yourselves know that we are appointed to this" (1 Thessalonians 3:3). They also quoted Hebrews 12:2 and called the believers to look "unto Jesus, the author and finisher of our faith, who for the joy that was set before Him endured the cross, despising the shame."

The Underground Church openly opposed the atheistic poisoning of youth in Rostov and Moscow—and all across Russia. They fought against the Communist poison and against the treacherous leaders of the official church, about which they write in one of their secret manifestos: "In our day, Satan dictates and 'the church' accepts all the decisions which are contrary to the commandments of God" (quoted in *Pravda Ukraini* of October 4, 1966).

Pravda Vostoka published the trial proceedings against the brethren Alexei Neverov, Boris Garmashov, and Axen Zubov, who organized groups to listen to gospel broadcasts from America. They recorded these messages on tapes, which they circulated afterward.

They were also accused of having organized secret gospel meetings under the forms of "excursions" and "artistic circles." Thus the Underground Church works just as the Early Church worked in the catacombs of Rome.

Sovietskaia Moldavia of September 15, 1966, wrote that the Underground Church mimeographed booklets. They gathered in public places, although this was forbidden by law, and went from place to place to witness for Christ.

This same newspaper recounts that on the train from Reni to Chisinau, three young boys and four girls sang a Christian hymn, "Let us dedicate our youth to Christ." The reporter professed himself revolted, because these believers preach "on the streets, in stations, in trains, buses, and even in state institutions." Again this was the Underground Church at work in Russia during the Communist era.

When at the trial of these Christians the sentence was announced for the crime of singing Christian hymns in public, the condemned fell on their knees and said, "We surrender ourselves into the hands of God. We thank thee, Lord, that Thou hast allowed us to suffer for this faith." Then the audience, led by the "fanatic" Madan, sang in the courtroom the hymn for which their brethren had just been sentenced to prison and torture.

On the first of May, the Christians of the villages Copceag and Zaharovka, having no churches, organized a secret service in the forest. They also organized meetings under the pretense of having a birthday party. (Many Christian families with four or five members had thirty-five "birthdays" a year as a cover for secret meetings.)

Neither prison nor torture can frighten the Christians of the Underground Church. Just as in the Early Church, persecution only deepens their dedication.

Pravda Ukraini of October 4, 1966, said about Brother Prokofiev—one of the leaders of the Russian Underground Church—that he had already been in prison three times, but as soon as he was released, he began to organize secret Sunday schools again and was re-arrested. He wrote in a secret manifesto: "Submitting to the human regulations [the Communist laws], the official church has deprived itself of the blessing of God."

And never imagine a prison as in the West when you hear about a sentenced brother in a restricted nation. Prison there means starvation, torture, and brainwashing.

Nauka i Religia (Science and Religion) No. 9 of 1966 reported that the Christians spread gospel literature inside the covers of *Ogoniok*—a periodical like *Look* or *Time.* They also handed out books that had the cover of *Anna Karenina* (a novel by Leo Tolstoy), but inside had a portion of the Bible.

In addition, the believers sang Christian songs in public. To the tune of "The Communist International," they sang words praising Christ (*Kazakstanskaia Pravda*, June 30, 1966).

In a secret letter published in Kulunda (Siberia), Christians say that the official "Baptist" leadership, "has destroyed the church and its true servants in the world, in the same way as the high priests, scribes, and Pharisees betrayed Jesus Christ to Pilate." But the faithful Underground Church works on!

The Bride of Christ continues to serve Him. The Communists themselves admitted that the Underground Church won Communists for Christ. They can be won!

Bakinskii Rabochi (The Worker of Baku) of April 27, 1966, reproduced a letter from Tania Ciugunova (a member of the Communist Youth Organization) who was won to Christ. This letter was seized by the Communist authorities:

> Dear Aunt Nadia,
>
> I send you blessings from our beloved Lord. Aunt Nadia, *how much He loves me!* We are nothing before Him. Aunt Nadia, I believe that you understand these words: "Love your enemies, bless them that curse you, do good to them that hate you and pray for them which despitefully use you."

Once this letter was seized, Peter Serebrennikov, the brother who brought her and many other young Communists to Christ, was sent to prison. The Communist newspaper quoted from one of his sermons: "We must believe our Savior as the first Christians did. For us the principal law is the Bible. We recognize nothing else. We must hurry to save men from sin, especially the youth." He stated that the Soviet law forbids telling youth about Christ, adding: "For us the only law is the Bible"—a very normal answer where a cruel atheistic dictatorship rules the country.

The Communist newspaper then described a "savage" picture: "Young boys and girls sing spiritual hymns. They receive the ritual baptism and keep the evil, treacherous teaching of love toward the enemy." The article also stated that many young boys and girls who carry membership in the Communist Youth Organization are in reality Christians! It concluded with the words: "How powerless must be the Communist school, how boresome and deprived of light … that the pastors are able to snatch away its disciples from under the nose of their indifferent educators."

In *Kazakstanskaia Pravda* of June 30, 1966, Communists expressed horror upon discovering that the pupil with the best grades was a Christian boy!

Kirgizskaia Pravda of January 17, 1966, quoted an underground Christian leaflet to mothers: "Let us join our efforts and prayers to dedicate to God the lives of our children from the time they are in the cradle! … Let us save our children from the influence of the world."

These efforts have been successful. The Communist newspapers bear witness to the fact that Christianity advanced among the youth!

A newspaper of Chiliabinsk, Russia, described how a Young Communist Organization girl, Nina, became a Christian by entering a secret Christian gathering.

Sovietskaia Justitia No. 9 of 1966 describes such an underground meeting. "It is held at midnight. Hidden, wary even of their own shadow, men came from different parts. The brethren filled the dark room, which has a very low ceiling. They were so many that there was no place to kneel. Because of the lack of air, the light in the primitive gas-lamp went out. Sweat ran from the faces of those present. On the street, one of the servants of the Lord was watching for policemen." Nina said that in such an assembly she was received with embraces, warmth, and care. "They had, as I have now, a great and enlightening faith—a faith in God. He takes us under His protection. Let the Komsomols who know me pass near me without greeting me! Let them look at me with despite and call me, as if slapping me, 'Baptist!' Let them do so! I don't need them."

So many other young Communists, like her, have made the decision to serve Christ to the end.

Kazakstanskaia Pravda of August 18, 1967, described the trial of the brethren Klassen, Bondar, and Teleghin. We are not told what sentence was given to them, but their crime was proclaimed: they had taught children about Christ.

Sovietskaia Kirghizia of June 15, 1967, complained that Christians "provoke the application of administrative measures against themselves." So the innocent Communist authorities, being continually provoked to arrest Christians by these obstinate

Christians themselves who are not content to remain free, have arrested another group. Their crime was having an illegal printing press, with fifteen hectographs and six bookbinding machines, on which Christian literature was printed.

Pravda of February 21, 1968, reported that thousands of women and girls were discovered wearing belts and ribbons on which Bible verses and prayers were printed. The authorities researched and found that the person who had launched this new fashion, which I could recommend also to the West, was none other than a Christian member of the Communist police, Brother Stasiuk of Liubertz. The newspaper announced his arrest.

The answers Christians of the Underground Church give, when brought before Communist courts, are divinely inspired. One judge demanded, "Why did you attract people to your forbidden sect?" A Christian sister answered, "Our aim is to win the *whole world* for Christ."

"Your religion is anti-scientific," the judge taunted at another trial, to which the accused girl—a student—answered, "Do you know more science than Einstein? Than Newton? They were believers. Our universe bears Einstein's name. I have learned in high school that its name is the Einsteinian universe. Einstein writes: 'If we cleanse the Judaism of the prophets and Christianity as Jesus has taught it from what came afterwards, especially from priestcraft, we have a religion which can save the world from all social evils. It is the holy duty of every man to do his utmost to bring this religion to triumph.' And remember our great physiologist Pavlov! Do not our books say that he was a Christian? Even Marx, in his preface to *Das Kapital*, said that 'Christianity, especially in its Protestant form, is the ideal religion for remaking characters destroyed by sin.' I had a character destroyed by sin. Marx has taught me to become a Christian in order to remake it. How can you, Marxists, judge me for this?"

It is easy to understand why the judge remained speechless.

To the same accusation of having an anti-scientific religion, a Christian answered before the court: "I am sure, Mr. Judge, that you are not such a great scientist as Simpson, the discoverer of chloroform and many other medicines. When asked which he considered to be his greatest discovery, he answered: 'It was not chloroform. My greatest discovery has been to know that I am a sinner and that I could be saved by the grace of God.'"

The life, the self-sacrifice, the blood that believers are ready to shed for their faith, is the greatest argument for Christianity presented by the Underground Church. It forms what the renowned missionary in Africa, Albert Schweitzer, called "the sacred fellowship of those who have the mark of pain"—the fellowship to which Jesus, the Man of Sorrows, belonged. The Underground Church is united by a bond of love toward its Savior. The same bond unites the members of the church with each other. No one in the world can defeat them.

In a letter smuggled out secretly, the Underground Church said, "We don't pray to be better Christians, but that we may be the only kind of Christians God means us to be: Christlike Christians, that is, Christians who bear willingly the cross for God's glory."

With the wisdom of serpents, according to the teaching of Jesus, the Christians always refused to identify their leaders when questioned before the court.

Pravda Vostoka (The Truth of the East) of January 15, 1966, told how defendant Maria Sevciuk responded when asked who had brought her to Christ: "God attracted me in His congregation." Another, when asked, "Who is your leader?" responded, "We have no human leader."

Christian children were asked, "Who has taught you to leave the Pioneers and to take off the red necktie?" They answered, "We have done it out of our free will. No one taught us."

Although in some places the tip of the "iceberg" showed, in other places, Christians practiced self-baptism to prevent the arrest of their leaders. Sometimes baptisms took place in a river, with the baptizer and the baptized both wearing masks so that no one could identify them in photographs.

Uchitelskaia Gazeta of January 30, 1964, told of an atheistic lecture in the village Voronin, of the district Volnecino-Korskii. As soon as the lecturer finished, "The believers began to publicly attack the atheistic teaching through questions," which the atheistic lecturer could not answer. They asked, "Where do you Communists get the moral principles you proclaim, but do not obey—such as 'don't steal' and 'don't kill'?" The Christians showed the lecturer that every such principle came from the Bible against which the Communists fight. The lecturer was entirely confused and the lecture finished with a victory for the believers!

Persecution of the Underground Church Grows

Christians in some of the former Soviet Republics are still persecuted today. In restricted nations worldwide, the Christians of the Underground Church are suffering today more than ever before. It is estimated that approximately 160,000 Christians were martyred in 1997. For Christians it is heartbreaking to know about the oppression of Jews in Communist countries. But the principal target of persecution is the Underground Church. Years ago, the Soviet press reported a wave of mass arrests and trials. In one place, eighty-two Christians were placed in an asylum for madmen. Twenty-four died after a few days because of "prolonged prayer"! Since when does lengthy prayer kill? Can you imagine what they went through?

The worst suffering imposed upon them was that, if it was discovered that they taught their children about Christ, their children were taken away from them for life—with no visitation rights.

During the Communist era, the Soviet Union signed the United Nations declaration "against discrimination in the sphere of education," which stipulated: "Parents must have the right to assure the religious and moral education of the children according to their own convictions." In one article, traitor Karev, who was the leader of the official Baptist Union of the Soviet Union, assured that this right was a reality in Russia—and fools believed him! Now, listen to what the Soviet press said.

In its June 4, 1963, issue, *Sowjetskaia Russia* recounted how a Baptist woman named Makrinkowa had her six children taken away from her, because she shared with them the Christian faith and forbade them to wear the Pioneer necktie.

When she heard the sentence, she said only, "I suffer for the faith." She had to pay for the boarding of her children who were taken away from her, so they could be poisoned with atheism. Christian mothers, think of her agony!

Uchitelskaia Gazeta reported that the same thing happened to Ignatii Mullin and his wife. The judge demanded that they leave their faith: "Choose between God and your daughter. Do you choose God?" The father answered, "I will not give up my faith."

Paul says, "All things work together for good" (Romans 8:28). I have seen such children who were raised as Christians and taken from their parents and put in Communist schools. Instead of being poisoned by atheism, the faith they had learned at home was spread to the other children!

The Bible says that "he who loves son or daughter more than Me is not worthy of Me" (Matthew 10:37). These words have meaning in captive nations.

Try to live a week without seeing your children! Then you will know the sufferings of our brethren in restricted nations. According to the March 29, 1967, issue of *Znamia Iunosti*, Mrs. Sitsh's son, Vsetsheslav, was taken away simply because she brought him up in the fear of the Lord. Mrs. Zabavina of Habarovsk was deprived of her orphaned granddaughter Tania because she had given her an "unnatural [Christian] education" (*Sovietskaia Rossia* of January

13, 1968). Depriving Christians of parental rights continues even today in restricted nations.

It would be unfair to speak only about the Protestant Underground Church.

The Orthodox Christians in Russia were completely changed. Millions of them have passed through prisons, where they had no beads, no crucifixes, no holy images, no incense, and no candles. The laymen were in prison without an ordained priest. The priests had no robes, no wheat bread, no wine to consecrate, no holy oils, no books with prepared prayers to be read. And they discovered that they could get by without all these things, by going to God directly in prayer. They began to pray and God began to pour forth His Spirit upon them. A genuine spiritual awakening, very similar to fundamental Christianity, took place among the Orthodox in Russia under communism.

So it happened that in Russia, as well as in the satellite countries, there existed an Orthodox Underground, which was in reality evangelical, fundamental, and very close to God. It kept, only by the power of habit, a very little of the Orthodox ritual. This Orthodox Underground has also given great martyrs. Who could say what happened to the aged Archbishop Yermogen of Kaluga? He dared to protest against the treacherous collaboration between the Patriarchy and the godless Communist government.

During seven decades of Communist rule until the end of the Soviet Union in the early '90s, the Russian press was full of the triumph of the Underground Church. It passed through unspeakable hardships but remained faithful ... and grew!

We in Romania sowed the seed by our secret work in the Russian army. So had others in Russia and in other countries invaded by the Russians. That seed has borne much fruit.

Communist Asia and other captive nations can be won for Christ. Our adversaries can become Christians! So can those oppressed by them, if only we will help them.

The proof that I am right is that the Underground Church flourished under communism in the Soviet Union, is flourishing in Communist Asia, and is growing in the Middle East today.

To show the beauty of our fellow Christians under terrible circumstances, I give below a few letters from Russian girls, the last two written in Russian prisons.

How a Communist Girl Found Christ

Following are three letters from Maria, a Christian girl who led Varia, a member of the Communist Youth Organization, to Christ.

First letter

… I continue to live here. I am very beloved. I am beloved also by a member of the cell of the Komsomol [the Communist Youth Organization]. She told me, "I cannot understand what a being you are. Here many insult and hurt you and yet you love all." I answered that God has taught us to love all, not only friends, but also enemies. Before, this girl did much harm to me, but I prayed for her with special concern. When she asked me if I can love her, too, I embraced her and we both began to weep. Now, we pray together.

Please, pray for her. Her name is Varia.

When you listen to those who loudly deny God, it seems that they really mean it. But life shows that many of them, although they curse God with their lips, in their hearts have a great longing. And you hear the groaning of the heart ... They seek something and wish to cover their inner emptiness with their godlessness.

Your sister in Christ, Maria

Second letter

In my former letter I wrote you about the atheist girl, Varia. Now I hurry to tell you, my beloved ones, about our great joy: Varia has received Christ as her personal Savior, witnessing openly to everyone about this.

When she believed in Christ and knew the gladness of salvation, she, at the same time, felt very unhappy. She was unhappy, because before she had propagated that there is no God. Now she has decided to atone for her guilt.

We went together to the assembly of the godless. Although I warned her to be reserved, it was useless. Varia went and I went with her to see what would happen. After the common singing of the Communist hymn (singing in which Varia did not participate), she came forward before the whole assembly. Courageously and with much feeling, she witnessed to those gathered about Christ as her Savior and asked her former comrades for forgiveness that she had had her spiritual eyes closed until then and had not seen that she herself was going to perdition and leading others toward it. She implored all to give up the way of sin and to come to Christ.

All became silent and no one interrupted her. When she finished speaking, she sang with her splendid voice the whole Christian hymn: "I am not ashamed to proclaim the Christ who died to defend His commandments and the power of His cross."

And afterwards ... afterwards they took away our Varia.

Today it is the ninth of May. We know nothing about her. But God is powerful to save her. Pray!

Your Maria

Third letter

Yesterday, the second of August, I had a talk in prison with our beloved Varia. My heart bleeds when I think about her. In fact she is still a child. She is only nineteen years of age. As a believer in the Lord, she is also a spiritual babe. But she loves the Lord with all her heart and went at once on the difficult way. The poor girl is so hungry. When we knew that she was in prison, we began to send her parcels. But she received only little of what was sent to her.

When I saw her yesterday, she was thin, pale, beaten. Only the eyes shone with the peace of God and with an unearthly joy.

Yes, my dear ones, those who have not experienced the wonderful peace of Christ cannot understand it ... But how happy are those who have this peace … For us who are in Christ no sufferings and frustrations should stop us …

I asked through the iron bars: "Varia, don't you regret what you did?" "No," she answered. "And if they would free me, I would go again and would tell them about the great love of Christ. Don't think that I suffer. I am very glad that the Lord loves me so much and gives me the joy to endure for His name."

I beg that you pray for her. She will probably be sent to Siberia. They have taken away her clothes and all of her things. She has remained without anything, except what is on her. She has no relatives and we must collect for the most necessary things. I have put apart the last sum which you sent me. If Varia is deported, I will hand it to her. I believe that God will strengthen her and will give her power to endure in the future, too. May God keep her!

Your Maria

Fourth letter

Dear Maria, at last I am able to write you. We arrived well at [location omitted]. Our camp is ten miles from town. I cannot describe our life. You know it. I wish to write only a little about me. I thank God that He gives me health and that I can work physically. Sister X and I were put to work in a workshop where we work at machines. The work is difficult and Sister X's health is bad. I must work for both her and me. I finish my work first and then I help my sister. We work twelve to thirteen hours a day. Our food is just as yours, very scarce. But it is not about this that I wished to write to you.

My heart praises and thanks God that, through you, He showed me the way to salvation. Now, being on this way, my life has a purpose and I know where to go and for whom I suffer. I feel the desire to tell and to witness to everybody about the great joy of salvation that I have in my heart. Who can separate us from the love of God in Christ? Nobody and nothing. Neither prison nor suffering. The sufferings that God sends us only strengthen us more and more in the faith in Him. My heart is so full that the grace of God overflows. At work, they curse and punish me, giving me extra work because I cannot be silent. I must tell everyone what the Lord has done for me. He has made me a new being, a new creation, of me who was on the way of perdition. Can I be silent after this? No, never! As long as my lips can speak, I will witness to every one about His great love.

On the way to the camp, we met with many brethren and sisters in Christ. How amazing it is that you feel through the Spirit that they are children of God when you first see the brethren and the sisters. It is useless to speak. From the first look you feel and know who they are.

While we were on the way to the camp, at one railway station, a woman came, gave us food and said only two words: "God lives."

The first evening when we arrived here (it was late), we were taken to underground barracks. We greeted those present with the words, "Peace with you." To our great joy, from all corners we heard the answer, "We receive you with peace." And from the first evening we felt that we are in a family.

Yes, it was really so. Here there are many who believe in Christ as their personal Savior. More than half of the prisoners are believers.

We have among us great singers and good preachers of the gospel. In the evening, when we all gather after heavy work, how wonderful it is to pass at least some time together in prayer at the feet of our Savior. With Christ there is freedom everywhere. I learned here many beautiful hymns and every day God gives me more and more of His Word. At the age of nineteen, I celebrated the birthday of Christ for the first time. Never will I forget this wonderful day! We had to work the whole day long. But some of our brethren were able to go to the river nearby. There they broke the ice and prepared the place where, during the night—according to the Word of God—seven brethren and I were baptized. Oh, how happy I am and how I would like that you, Maria, should be with me, too, that I may atone at least a little bit, through my love toward you for the wrong I committed in times past against you. But God puts every one of us in His place and we must stand firm where God has put us.

Give greetings to the whole family of God's children. God will richly bless your common work, as He blessed me, too. Read Hebrews 12:1–3.

All our brethren greet you and are glad that your faith in God is so powerful and that you praise Him in your sufferings unceasingly. If you write to others, tell them our greetings.

Yours, Varia

Fifth letter

Dear Maria, at last I have found the opportunity to write you a few lines. I can tell you, my dear one, that, by the grace of God,

Sister X and I are healthy and feel well. We are now in [location omitted].

I thank you for your motherly care for me. We received all you have prepared for us. I thank you for the most valuable thing, the Bible. Thanks to all. When you write to them, send my greetings and thanks for what they have done for me.

Since the Lord revealed to me the deep mystery of His holy love, I consider myself to be the happiest in the world. The persecutions that I have to endure I consider as a special grace. I am glad that the Lord gave me from the first days of my faith the great happiness to suffer for Him. Pray for me that I may remain faithful to the Lord to the end.

May the Lord keep you all and strengthen you for the holy battle!

Sister X and I kiss you all. When we are sent to [location omitted] perhaps we will have the opportunity to write to you again. Don't worry about us. We are glad and joyful, because our reward in heaven is great (Matthew 5:11,12).

Your Varia

This is the last letter from Varia—the young Communist girl who found Christ, witnessed about Him, and was sentenced to slave labor. She was never heard from again, but her beautiful love and witness for Christ shows the spiritual beauty of the suffering, faithful Underground Church.

Chapter 7

_____

How Western Christians Can Help

I have been called the "Voice of the Underground Church." I do not feel worthy to be the voice of such an honored part of the Body of Christ.

However, in Communist nations, I led for years a part of the Underground Church. By a miracle I survived fourteen years of torture and imprisonment, including two years in a prison "dying room." By an even greater miracle, God somehow saw fit to reach into the prison and bring me out. It was decided by the Underground Church in Romania that I should leave my country and take a message to the free Christians of the world. By a miracle, my family and I were able to leave, and I was able to fulfill the charge given me by those who remained behind laboring, risking, suffering, and dying in dozens of captive nations.

I speak on behalf of my brethren who lie in countless nameless graves. I speak on behalf of my brethren who now meet secretly in forests, basements, attics, and other such places.

The message I bring from the Underground Church is:

"Don't abandon us!"

"Don't forget us!"

"Don't write us off!"

"Give us the tools we need! We will pay the price for using them!"

This is the message I have been charged to deliver to the free Church.

I speak for the Underground Church, the silenced Church, the "dumb" Church, which has no voice to speak.

Hear the cries of your brothers and sisters in captive nations! They do not ask for escape, safety, or an easy life. They ask only for the tools to counteract the poisoning of their youth—the next generation—with atheism. They ask for Bibles to use in spreading the Word of God. How can they spread the Word of God if they do not have it?

The Underground Church is like a surgeon who was traveling by train. The train collided with another train and hundreds of people lay on the ground, mangled, injured, dying. The surgeon walked among the dying, crying out: "If only I had my tools! If only I had my tools!" With these surgical instruments he could have saved many lives. He had the willingness ... but he did not have the tools. This is where the Underground Church stands. It is *so willing* to give its all. It is *so willing* to give its martyrs! It is *so willing* to risk years in prisons! But all of its willingness is of no value if it does not have the tools with which to work. The plea of the faithful, courageous Underground Church to you who are free is: "Give us the tools—the Gospels, the Bibles, the literature, the help—and we will do the rest!"

How Christians in the Free World Can Help

Every Christian in the free world can help at once in the following ways.

Atheists are men who do not acknowledge the invisible sources of their life. They have no sense for what is mystery in the universe and in life. Christians can help them best by walking themselves not by sight, but by faith, leading a life of fellowship with the invisible God.

They can help us best by leading the lives of consistent Christians, lives of sacrifice. They can help by protesting publicly as often as Christians are persecuted.

Western Christians can help us by praying for the persecutors that they may be saved. Such a prayer may seem naive. We prayed for the Communists and they tortured us the next day even worse than before the prayer. But the prayer of the Lord in Jerusalem was also "naive." They crucified Him after this prayer. But only a few days later, they beat their breasts and five thousand were converted in one day.

For the others, too, the prayer was not lost. Any prayer that is not accepted by the one for whom you intercede returns to you with great blessings. Fulfilling the word of Christ, many other

Christians and I always prayed for Hitler and his men. And I am sure that our prayer helped to defeat him as much as the bullets of the allied soldiers.

We must love our neighbors as ourselves. Communists and other persecutors are our neighbors as much as anyone else.

They are the result of our not making known the words of Christ: "I have come that they may have life, and that they may have it more abundantly" (John 10:10). Christians have not yet made this abundant life available to everyone. They have left some on the fringe of everything valuable in life. These individuals have rebelled and constituted the Communist Party and other false beliefs. Often the victims of social injustice themselves, they are now bitter and cruel. We have to fight against them. But Christians, even if they fight against an enemy, understand and love him.

We are not guiltless of the fact that some live in rebellion. We are guilty at least by neglect of duty.

For this we have to atone by loving them—which is something entirely different from liking them—and praying for them.

I am not so naive as to believe that love alone can solve these problems. I would not advise the authorities of a state to solve the problem of gangsterism only by love. There must be a police force, judges, and prisons for gangsters—not just pastors. If gangsters do not repent, they must be jailed. I would never use the Christian phrase about "love" to counteract the appropriate political, economic, or cultural fight against Communists and other tyrants, who are nothing but gangsters on an international scale. Gangsters steal a purse; they steal whole countries.

But the pastor and the individual Christian have to do their best to bring to Christ rebellious nations—whatever crimes they commit—as well as their innocent victims. We have to pray for them with understanding.

Bibles Are Urgently Needed

Another way free Christians can help is by sending Bibles and Bible portions. Means exist by which they can be safely sent into restricted nations, if only free Christians will provide them for our brothers and sisters of the Underground Church. While still in Romania, I received many Bibles brought in by certain means. There is no question of the ways to send them—only that they must be provided.

They are desperately needed. Thousands of Christians have not seen Bibles or Gospels for decades in Communist nations such as China and North Korea.

Two very dirty villagers came to my home one day to buy a Bible. They had come from their village to take the job of shoveling the frozen earth all winter long to earn money in the slight hope that they might be able to buy an old, tattered Bible with it and take it back to their village. Because I had received Bibles from America, I was able to hand them a new Bible, not an old tattered one. They could not believe their eyes! They tried to pay me with the money they had earned. I refused their money. They rushed back to their village with the Bible. A few days later I received a letter of unrestrained, ecstatic joy thanking me for the Scriptures.

It was signed by thirty villagers! They had carefully cut the Bible into thirty parts and exchanged the parts with one another!

It was pathetic to hear a Russian begging for one page of the Bible to feed his soul. They were happy to exchange a cow or a goat for a Bible. One man traded his wedding ring for a battered New Testament. Many children have never seen a Christmas card. If they had one, all the children of the village would gather around it, and some old man might explain to them about the baby Jesus, his virgin birth, and the story of Christ and salvation. All this—from one Christmas card! We send Bibles, Gospels, and literature to Christians in these restricted nations. This is one way *you* can do something.

We also print and send special literature to counterattack the atheistic poison being given the youth from kindergarten to college. In the Soviet Union, the Communists prepared *The Atheist's Guidebook*, which is the atheist's "Bible." Simple versions are taught to kindergarten children, with more advanced versions of the same guidebook taught as the children progress. The evil "Bible" follows a child as he grows and advances—poisoning him with atheism all the way. We print and send *The Answer to the Atheist's Handbook* as the Christian answer to poisonous, atheistic teachings.

Our poisoned youth must have an answer—God's answer— the Christian answer—our answer! This is another thing you can do, by helping provide special literature to nations where God is "illegal." Such literature includes illustrated youth literature and children's Bibles.

We also must "join hands" with members of the Underground Church and give them the financial means to travel about with the gospel in person-to-person evangelism. So many of them are "chained" to their homes for lack of funds to use for travel tickets, and for food while traveling. Thus they are stranded, unable to move about while villages twenty to thirty miles away vainly call for them to come for secret meetings. By providing funds for them each month, we can "unchain" them to answer those calls and go to distant towns and villages with the Word of God. For example, we purchase motorcycles for Vietnamese and Chinese pastors who go to share the gospel in "forbidden areas" of their nations. We provide bicycles for evangelists in Muslim Bangladesh who witness at great risk.

Christian laymen and laywomen must have financial help. Being Christians, they earn barely enough to survive, leaving nothing with which to go from village to village with the gospel. This is the "miracle" a few dollars a month will do for them.

Pastors of official churches who conduct a secret, parallel ministry at great risk must have funds secretly provided them for such purposes. The willingness of these pastors to risk their freedom by ignoring regulations and preaching the gospel to children, youth, and adults in secret meetings is not enough. They must have the means to carry out their fruitful secret ministry. Giving funds for that purpose will help such a member of the Underground Church effectively spread the gospel.

Next, we must broadcast the gospel into captive nations by radio. Using stations in the free world, we can spiritually feed the Underground Church, which itself is in great need of the Bread of Life. Because the Communist governments use shortwave radio to disseminate their propaganda to their own people, millions of people in restricted nations have radios that will receive these broadcasts. Doors remain open to broadcast into captive nations by radio, and this work must be extended. The Underground Church must have the spiritual food these broadcasts provide. This is another way you can help the Underground Church in these restricted countries.

The Tragedy of Families of Christian Martyrs

The families of Christian martyrs also need our assistance. Tens of thousands of such families are now suffering in an indescribably tragic way. When a member of the Underground Church is arrested, a terrible tragedy strikes his family. It is usually illegal for anyone to help them. This is very well planned by the governments to increase the suffering of the wife and children left behind. When a Christian goes to prison—and often to torture or death—the suffering only begins. His family suffers endlessly. I can state for a fact that if rank-and-file Christians in the free world had not sent me and my family help, we would never have survived to write these words!

More martyrs are being made all the time. Though they go to their graves and to their reward, their families live in horribly tragic conditions. We can and must help them. Of course, we must also help starving Indians and Africans. But who deserves the help of Christians more than the families of those who have died for

Christ or who are tortured for their faith in prisons in restricted nations?

Since my release, The Voice of the Martyrs has already sent much help to families of Christian martyrs. What has been done is little in comparison to what we could do with your help.

My Message to You from the Underground Church

As a member of the Underground Church who has survived and escaped, I have brought you a message, an appeal, a plea from my brethren whom I have left behind.

They have sent me to deliver this message to you. Miraculously I have survived to deliver it.

I have told you of the urgency of bringing Christ to the Communist world and other captive nations. I have told you of the urgency of helping the families of Christian martyrs. I have told you of practical ways you can help the Underground Church fulfill its mission of spreading the gospel.

When I was beaten on the bottom of the feet, my tongue cried. Why did my tongue cry? It was not beaten. It cried because the tongue and feet are both part of the same body. And you free Christians are part of the same Body of Christ that is now beaten in prisons in restricted nations, that even now gives martyrs for Christ. Can you not feel our pain?

The Early Church in all of its beauty, sacrifice, and dedication has come alive again in these countries.

While our Lord Jesus Christ agonized in prayer in the Garden of Gethsemane, Peter, James, and John were a mere stone's throw away from the greatest drama of history—but they were deep in sleep. How much of your own Christian concern and giving is directed toward the relief of the martyr church? Ask your pastors and church leaders what is being done in your name to help your brothers and sisters in restricted nations around the world.

In these countries, the drama, bravery, and martyrdom of the Early Church are happening all over again—now—and the free Church sleeps.

Our brethren there, alone and without help, are waging the greatest, most courageous battle of the twentieth century, equal to the heroism, courage, and dedication of the Early Church. And the free Church sleeps on, oblivious of their struggle and agony, just as Peter, James, and John slept in the moment of their Savior's agony.

Will you also sleep while your brethren in Christ suffer and fight for the gospel?

Will you hear our message: "Remember us, help us"?

"Don't abandon us!"

Now I have delivered the message from the faithful, martyred Church—from *your* brothers and sisters suffering in the bonds of atheistic communism, and under attack across the world from Indonesia to Africa. Don't abandon them.

The Book That Shocked the World

Regarding his book *Tortured for Christ*, Richard Wurmbrand said, "[It] has no literary value. It was written in only three days shortly after my release from prison. But it was written with pen and tears. And for some reason, God has chosen to bless this writing and use it for His purpose." Since the book was first published in 1967, Richard's testimony has inspired millions across the globe.

After readers finished *Tortured for Christ*, letters poured into the Wurmbrands' mailbox. Readers said they were "shaken," "deeply struck," and "appalled at the account of your suffering." Others said that "it changed the course of my life" and that it "opened thousands of eyes to the truth about communism, as well as pointing many to Christ."

But getting it published was no simple task. It bore a message that many wanted to ignore. Richard was told by one publisher, "This book cannot sell. If published, it will do harm."

God had other plans for this book. Word spread about this "Iron Pastor." Copies of his book were shared among friends. Soon, it was translated into other languages, such as German, Dutch, Swedish, and Norwegian. People were appalled and shocked at what was happening to Christians in the Communist nations of Eastern Europe and the Soviet Union, also known as the countries behind the Iron Curtain. They began inviting Richard to speak in their churches and on the radio, exposing the atrocities of the Communists toward the Body of Christ.

Some Christian leaders called him a lunatic—one who had lost his mind in the confines of a solitary prison cell. Others accused him of exaggerating the truth and sensationalizing the stories of persecuted Christians behind the Iron Curtain. The *Sydney Morning Herald* wrote that he was "concerned to the point of obsession that the plight of Christian prisoners of conscience should not be forgotten." For Wurmbrand, he couldn't help but be obsessed with this message as he faced indifference in the West. "I have suffered more from the complacency of the West than from the Communists," he once said.

Richard could not remain silent. "When I left prison, I promised God that I would continue the life of a prisoner," he said. "I would never take a day off. I would work day and night for the Lord." Within his first year in the United States, Pastor Wurmbrand was detained twice for "disrupting" pro-Communist rallies. He was called to testify before the Senate, stripping to the waist to reveal the scars from the frequent tortures. "These are the scars of millions of Christians held in Communist jails today," he declared, "people who are being tortured to death."

There were many who listened. To them, Richard Wurmbrand became the "Iron Curtain Paul" and the "Voice of the Underground Church." A reporter with the *Philadelphia Herald* said of Wurmbrand, "He stood in the midst of lions, but they could not devour him." The *Indianapolis Star* wrote that he and his wife, Sabina, "were classified as enemies of the state and counterrevolutionaries, although their weapons were Bibles and their spy techniques were preaching God's word."

As Richard traveled the world, sharing the message of today's persecuted Christians, those individuals who were inspired by his message asked him what they could do to help. His response was simply, "Start a mission to help the persecuted. Inform churches about how their brothers and sisters are suffering." Soon affiliate offices were started in Australia, Canada, the Netherlands, Germany, and other countries. Others started their own ministries that focused on advancing the kingdom in some of the world's most hostile mission fields, such as Burma and Sudan. Even Christians in Vietnam read *Tortured for Christ* in the early 1970s to prepare them for what they would face when their country fell to Ho Chi Minh's Communists.

Not long after he wrote *Tortured for Christ*, Richard Wurmbrand published the first issue of *The Voice of the Martyrs* newsletter and began the organization known at that time as Jesus to the Communist World (later changed to The Voice of the Martyrs). In October 1967, with $100, an old typewriter, and five hundred names and addresses, he wrote about the testimonies and trials facing our brothers and sisters in Communist countries. "I started the organization … with a bad typewriter and a tape recorder," Wurmbrand told a journalist. "On the 28th of the month I did not know how I would pay my rent on the 30th, or how I would pay my telephone bill."

Readers would write to the Wurmbrands appalled at the atrocities he described. "How could this be true?" they asked. Others said the newsletter gave them nightmares and asked not to receive it. But those who looked beyond the sufferings and tortures saw a beauty—a beauty in the hearts of men, women, and even children who refused to renounce Christ. Readers witnessed a living faith that enabled men like Wurmbrand to "kiss the bars" of their prison cell, to rejoice in the fellowship of Christ's suffering.

Richard Wurmbrand looked beyond the temporal and into the eternal. He was a pastor first, an advocate second. He frequently challenged readers to be inspired by the stories of the persecuted, as he wrote in March 1974:

Our mission helps the families of martyrs in Communist countries, but it also serves as a reminder to Christians in the free world. Examine yourself. You are a Christian. But do you belong to the right category of Christians who understand that they must take up their cross daily and help others bear theirs? Do you know it is your duty to bear with patience, love, and joy the worst ordeals, even death under torture? I know you have your sorrow. Be like the sister of Victor Korbel [a Czech martyr] and sing, "Jesus, lover of my soul."

While not all of us may endure persecution as Richard Wurmbrand did, we should not be surprised when trials do come and we are tested in our faith. "We are not all called to such sufferings," he noted. "Martyrdom is the exception." Instead of despairing at the atrocities persecuted Christians were facing, he encouraged readers to rejoice that they have been considered worthy to suffer for Christ.

He knew the stories of courageous faith in the face of torture and death would benefit readers. "And now, what will you profit by reading the newsletter?" he once asked. "It will greatly enlarge your vision. Life is too short to be narrow. You need to enlarge your horizons, sharing the joys and sorrows of your fellowmen and having fellowship with angels, glorified saints, and God." So he chose Hebrews 13:3 as the biblical foundation of The Voice of the Martyrs' ministry: "Remember them that are in bonds, as bound with them; and them which suffer adversity, as being yourselves also in the body" (KJV).

Not long after communism in Eastern Europe and the Soviet Union began to collapse in 1989, Islamic extremist groups started to rise and have specifically targeted Christians. Their aim: to eradicate any Christian presence in their country. In 2014, the self-proclaimed Islamic State (ISIS) gave Christians in Mosul, Iraq, the ultimatum to convert to Islam, pay a high tax called a *jizya*, flee, or die. ISIS identified Christians' homes and businesses by marking them with the Arabic letter "N," or ن, that labeled them as "Nasara," or Nazarenes—how the Quran refers to Christians. Most Christians chose to flee to the nearby city of Erbil, where many are still living in refugee camps and makeshift shelters.

Other Islamic extremist groups like the Taliban have martyred Afghan believers and Westerners because they are followers of Christ. Boko Haram has terrorized northern Nigeria and Cameroon, maiming and slaughtering any Christian who refuses to deny Christ and turn to Islam.

Still, these persecuted members of Christ's Body have shown a supernatural resilience through the Holy Spirit who empowers them to refuse to deny their Savior, Jesus Christ. One woman in Nigeria whose Christian village was attacked by Boko Haram said, "I once thought that even if I should be captured by Boko Haram, I will never deny my faith in Christ Jesus. So when we met them, my mind was made up beforehand since I know Who I serve." When ISIS forced one man and his family to flee their home in Mosul, he said, "I was 100 percent sure I would receive this sword in my body at any moment. I totally believe I was so weak, but the Holy Spirit was with me to strengthen me to confront them and to tell them, 'I will not be Muslim.'"

It is difficult to comprehend that joy and courage can coexist with some of the worst sufferings known to man. But with God, all things are possible, and He causes all things to work together for good for those who love Him. For example, Muslims in the Middle East are turning to Christ after witnessing the harsh face of ISIS. And one of the fastest growing churches in the Muslim world is in Iran, where Ayatollah Ruhollah Khomeini's Islamic Revolution of 1979 has shown people the true nature of Islam.

Richard Wurmbrand labored to be a voice for our Christian brothers and sisters in chains until his death in 2001. His legacy compels us to be their voice and serve our persecuted family by providing help, Bibles, and ministry tools. This work comes with a cost. When asked by a newspaper reporter in 1971 about the risk of this work, Richard replied, "There is no work without risk ... It is a much greater risk to appear before God with the guilt of having allowed one-third of the world to perish without the knowledge of Jesus Christ. So we take all the risks." That risk remains true today. As Wurmbrand aptly stated in this book, persecuted members of Christ's Body plead with the West, saying, "Give us the tools we need! We will pay the price for using them!" The Voice of the Martyrs continues to serve our brothers and sisters who are persecuted for their witness in almost seventy nations around the world, while being their voice to inspire Christians in the West.

"It's too risky to sit in prison for twenty years for something that is not sure," said Richard Wurmbrand. "If you are willing to die for your faith, you must believe it." What will *you* do with the message in this book? Have you decided if following Jesus and being His witness will be worth it? Will you allow the testimonies of courageous faith to inspire you to have a deeper commitment to Christ and His Great Commission? Be inspired by our persecuted brothers and sisters. And join them in fellowship.

—*The Voice of the Martyrs*

Richard and Sabina Wurmbrand

Early photo of Richard and Sabina in Romania

Christian Wölfkes (pictured with his wife) was the village carpenter who led Richard Wurmbrand to Christ (see pp. 24–25). Wölfkes prayed, "My God, I have served you on earth and I wish to have my reward on earth as well as in heaven. And my reward should be that I should not die before I bring a Jew to Christ, because Jesus was from the Jewish people. But I am poor, old, and sick. I cannot go around and seek a Jew. In my village there are none. Bring a Jew into my village and I will do my best to bring him to Christ."

Before his arrest in 1948, Richard Wurmbrand served in the Romanian Lutheran Church in Bucharest. According to the Wurmbrands, including written accounts by Sabina, the church became a cartoon film studio. "Pews and the altar were torn out, and windows blocked," Sabina wrote. "In one way it was a blessing in disguise: it made our attic on the top floor of the block very difficult to watch closely. Studio technicians, musicians, secretaries, and so on came and went all day and couldn't be distinguished easily from our brethren." Churches were frequently closed under Communist rule and adapted for a variety of uses, such as public baths, planetariums, museums, factories, storage facilities, and swimming pools.

Richard Wurmbrand (back center) is pictured with several men from his church three years before his first imprisonment. To his immediate right is a Russian soldier whom Richard and Sabina led to Christ. To Richard's immediate left is Brother Moscovoci—the Wurmbrands' most beloved disciple. He later became their associate pastor and helped lead the church while Richard was in prison the first time, for seven years. He later betrayed Richard to the authorities, resulting in Richard's second arrest. Richard's last words to Sabina as he was taken away in a police van were, "Give all my love to ... the Pastor [Moscovoci], who betrayed me." After his release, Richard embraced him on the streets of Bucharest, expressing his forgiveness. The man standing in front of Richard was a missionary among the Jews who, along with the Wurmbrands, came within hours of being shot during World War II. The man pictured on Richard's far left is an evangelist who loved the Wurmbrands and whose ministry was greatly influenced by Richard's example.

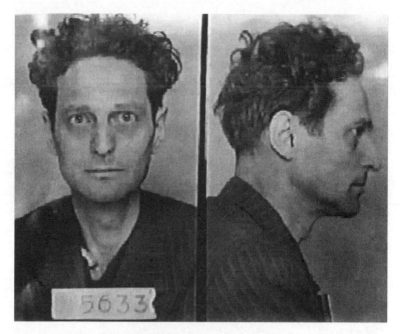

Prison mugshot of Richard Wurmbrand after he was kidnapped off the streets of Bucharest on Feb. 29, 1948, and imprisoned by the Communist secret police under a false name.

Prison mugshot of Richard Wurmbrand taken in 1951 at the Tirgu-Ocna prison in Romania.

Jilava Prison, pictured here, is one of the prisons where Richard Wurmbrand was held.

Another prison where Richard Wurmbrand was held from 1960 to 1964 was Gherla, pictured here.

Richard after his release from prison.

Richard and Sabina are pictured with two friends. This photo is believed to have been taken in the Wurmbrands' upstairs apartment.

A cover of secret police interrogation and surveillance folders, such as those kept for Richard and Sabina Wurmbrand. Richard's file contained thousands of pages.

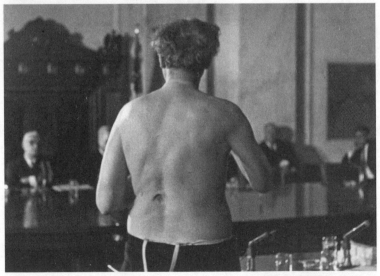

In May 1966, Richard stripped to the waist before a U.S. Senate Sub-Committee to show the scars caused by torture he endured in Communist prisons. To read an excerpt from the hearing, see the Appendix, page 193.

This photo of an underground baptism in Novosibirsk, Russia, was published in VOM's June 1970 newsletter. Richard wrote that many of the Christians in the picture were in jail, as authorities surprised them at the baptismal service.

An Underground Church gathering in Communist Russia. Believers sometimes met in the woods so their meeting could be disguised as a picnic or other celebration.

Christians smuggling Bibles into Communist Eastern Europe passed through checkpoints like this one. Here, an East German policeman checks a car at the border. This photo was published in VOM's June 1970 newsletter.

Why Didn't the Washington Press Let Nation's Editors Know of This ?

Rev. Richard Wurmbrand (above) at Pentagon being interviewed. (Below), he speaks to crowd and shows scars inflicted by reds with knives and flame.

Patriotic demonstrator on Pentagon grounds, in automotive, hydraulic basket lift called "cherrypicker," in which the Rev. Wurmbrand also appeared. This was ignored by press and radio-TV.

Richard Wurmbrand climbed into a boom lift "cherry picker" and preached the gospel to pro-communist youth in Washington, D.C., on Oct. 21, 1967. He showed the jeering crowd his scars inflicted by the communists.

In December 1989, Communist rule came to an end in Romania with the execution of the country's dictator, Nicolae Ceausescu. Soon afterward, the Wurmbrands returned to Romania for a visit. "This is the happiest day of my life!" Richard exclaimed. He and Sabina embraced in front of Ceausescu's palace, which was built directly over the underground prison where Richard was incarcerated.

During the Wurmbrands' return trip to Romania, Richard visited a facility where VOM books and Bibles were being stored. It was in the same area where Richard had been held in solitary confinement, under Ceausescu's newly built palace. Caraman (pictured on Richard's right in the photo) was also kept in a solitary cell in this same location. While in prison, Richard and Caraman dreamed about distributing books if ever they were free—a seeming impossibility.

Sabina Wurmbrand was also arrested. She was held in the prison of Codlea and sentenced to forced labor on the Danube Canal. She is pictured here with Caraman (on her left) and another friend of the ministry at the abandoned canal project.

As Richard and Sabina traveled the world sharing stories about persecuted Christians, people often asked what they could do to help. Richard's response was simply, "Start a mission." Many heeded those words, and years later the International Christian Association (ICA) was founded to help coordinate work among all the missions started as a result of the Wurmbrands' testimony. Today, the ICA continues to help all of these missions share stories and collaborate on international projects on behalf of persecuted Christians.

The Wurmbrands traveled extensively and tirelessly throughout the world, sharing the message of persecuted Christians. Sabina passed away in 2000, and Richard in 2001. Top picture taken in India; bottom picture taken in South Africa.

Appendix

Excerpt from Senate Subcommittee Hearing

"Communist Exploitation of Religion"

Congressional Testimony of Richard Wurmbrand at the Hearing Before the Subcommittee to Investigate the Administration of the Internal Security Act and Other Internal Security Laws, of the Committee on the Judiciary United States Senate.

MAY 6, 1966

SENATOR DODD. I have many more questions, but would you show your wounds and scars, if you have some?

REVEREND WURMBRAND. I apologize here before the ladies.

SENATOR DODD. Take your time. If ever a man was entitled to time, I think you are.

REVEREND WURMBRAND. Look here, look here, look here. Look here, look here. And so the whole body.

SENATOR DODD. What is the scar behind your ear?

REVEREND WURMBRAND. Here they put the knife and said, "Give accusatory statements against your bishops and against the other pastors. Do you give or not?" And they cut. It is true that they did not cut very deeply.

SENATOR DODD. These are all knife wounds?

REVEREND WURMBRAND. They tortured by all means. They beat until they broke the bones. They used red hot irons, they used knives, they used everything. And what was the first thing is not that they beat, not what they did, but how they did it. They interrogated you very politely, and if you did not wish to say what they asked they said, "Well, we have the first. On the 15th you will be beaten and tortured at 10 o'clock in the evening." Imagine what 14 days were after this. We have had prisoners who during this time, which has been given to them, knocked at the door, "I can't bear it. I will say everything," before they have been tortured.

SENATOR DODD. I wish you would turn around before you put your shirt on.

REVEREND WURMBRAND. And that it may be very clear, it is not that I boast with these marks. I show to you the tortured body of my country, of my fatherland, and of my church, and they appeal to the American Christians and to all freemen of America to think about our tortured body, and we do not ask you to help us. We ask you only one thing. Do not help our oppressors and do not praise them. You cannot be a Christian and praise the inquisitors of Christians. That is what I have to say.

SENATOR DODD. All right. You may put on your clothes. That scar on your right breast, do you remember how that was inflicted?

REVEREND WURMBRAND. Yes; by knife.

SENATOR DODD. By knife?

REVEREND WURMBRAND. By knife. I have been in Oslo. I went to a hospital. There were several physicians. I can give their names. Spoke with them about religion. In the beginning they said, "We are atheists," and then they saw my body and I asked them what treatment do I need. They said: "About treatment, do not ask us. Ask only the one in whom we don't believe, but who has kept you alive, because according to our medical books, you are dead. A man who has what you have, with four vertebras broken, cannot live. According to our medical books, you are dead. If you are alive, then the one in whom we don't believe has kept you alive."

Resources about the Persecuted Church

Other Books by Richard Wurmbrand

With God in Solitary Confinement
The Oracles of God
In God's Underground
100 Prison Meditations
Christ on the Jewish Road
The Overcomers
Victorious Faith
Alone with God
Reaching Toward the Heights
If Prison Walls Could Speak
Proofs of God's Existence
The Answer to the Atheist's Handbook
Marx & Satan
The Midnight Bride (formerly *The Sweetest Song*)
The Pastor's Wife (by Sabina Wurmbrand)

Other Books by The Voice of the Martyrs

Extreme Devotion
Hearts of Fire
Jesus Freaks, by DC Talk and The Voice of the Martyrs
Foxe: Voices of the Martyrs
Iran: Desperate for God
Into the Den of Infidels
Saul to Paul
I Am N

Videos by The Voice of the Martyrs

Tortured for Christ (The Movie). The dramatic testimony of Pastor Richard Wurmbrand as told in the international bestseller *Tortured for Christ*. Limited theatrical release spring 2018. Visit torturedforchrist.com for news, updates, and ways to get involved.

Richard & Sabina Wurmbrand Documentary. After spending years in Communist prisons, Richard and Sabina Wurmbrand emerged with an incredible story of faith and undying love found in the midst of suffering. Their story shocked the Western world and led to the ministry of The Voice of the Martyrs. Now you can witness their incredible journey through a new 50-minute documentary as they share, in their own words, what God has accomplished. Viewing this DVD, which contains never-before-seen footage from VOM archives, Romania, and the Wurmbrand library, will lead you to a deeper understanding of how persecution can refine the faith of the believer.

Their suffering, often horrific, was real. Their struggles, painful and long. But hope prevailed. Be inspired by the incredible story of Richard and Sabina Wurmbrand and gain a deeper understanding of their passion for those who are persecuted for their faith in Jesus Christ.

About the Author

Pastor Richard Wurmbrand (1909–2001) was an evangelical minister who endured fourteen years of Communist imprisonment and torture in his homeland of Romania. Few names are better known in Romania, where he is one of the most widely recognized Christian leaders, authors, and educators.

In 1945, when the Communists seized Romania and attempted to control the churches for their purposes, Richard Wurmbrand immediately began an effective, vigorous "underground" ministry to his enslaved people as well as the invading Russian soldiers. He was arrested in 1948, along with his wife, Sabina. His wife was a slave-laborer for three years on the Danube Canal. Richard Wurmbrand spent three years in solitary confinement, seeing no one but his Communist torturers. He was then transferred to a group cell, where the torture continued for five more years.

Due to his international stature as a Christian leader, diplomats of foreign embassies asked the Communist government about his safety and were informed that he had fled Romania. Secret police, posing as released fellow-prisoners, told his wife of attending his burial in the prison cemetery. His family in Romania and his friends abroad were told to forget him because he was dead.

After eight-and-a-half years in prison, he was released and immediately resumed his work with the Underground Church. A couple of years later, in 1959, he was re-arrested and sentenced to twenty-five years in prison.

Pastor Wurmbrand was released in a general amnesty in 1964, and again continued his underground ministry. Realizing the great danger of a third imprisonment, Christians in Norway negotiated with the Communist authorities for his release from Romania. The Communist government had begun "selling" their political prisoners. The "going price" for a prisoner was $1,900; the price for Wurmbrand was $10,000.

In May 1966, he testified before the U.S. Senate's Internal Security Subcommittee and stripped to the waist to show the scars of eighteen deep torture wounds covering his torso. His story was carried around the world in newspapers throughout the U.S., Europe, and Asia. Wurmbrand was warned in September 1966 that the Communist regime of Romania planned to assassinate him; yet he was not silent in the face of this death threat.

Founder of the Christian mission The Voice of the Martyrs, he and his wife traveled throughout the world establishing a network of over thirty offices that provide relief to the families of imprisoned Christians in Islamic nations, Communist Vietnam, China, and other countries where Christians are persecuted for their faith. His message has been, "Hate the evil systems, but love your persecutors. Love their souls, and try to win them for Christ."

Pastor Wurmbrand authored numerous books, which have been translated into over seventy languages throughout the world. Christian leaders have called him the "Voice of the Underground Church" and "the Iron Curtain Paul."

The Voice of the Martyrs is a nonprofit, inter-denominational Christian missions organization dedicated to serving our persecuted family world-wide through practical and spiritual assistance and leading other members of the Body of Christ into fellowship with them. VOM was founded in 1967 by Pastor Richard Wurmbrand, who was imprisoned fourteen years in Communist Romania for his faith in Christ. His wife, Sabina, was imprisoned for three years. In 1965, Richard and Sabina were ransomed out of Romania and established a global network of missions dedicated to assisting persecuted Christians.

Be inspired by the courageous faith of our persecuted brothers and sisters in Christ and learn ways to serve them by subscribing to VOM's free monthly newsletter. Visit us at persecution.com or call 1-800-747-0085.

Explore VOM's five main purposes and statement of faith at: persecution.com/aboutvom.

To learn more about VOM's work, please contact us:

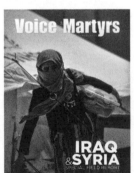

United States	persecution.com
Australia	vom.com.au
Belgium	hvk-aem.be
Canada	vomcanada.com
Czech Republic	hlas-mucedniku.cz
Finland	marttyyrienaani.fi
Germany	verfolgte-christen.org
Italy	eun.ch
The Netherlands	sdok.org
New Zealand	vom.org.nz
South Africa	persecution.co.za
South Korea	vomkorea.kr
United Kingdom	releaseinternational.org

Response Form

○ I would like to receive a free subscription to *The Voice of the Martyrs* monthly newsletter.

○ Please send me more information on how I can help the persecuted church.

○ I already receive *The Voice of the Martyrs* newsletter. Please send a subscription to my friend at the address below. (Please include your name: _____. We do not accept anonymous referrals.)

○ I have received Jesus Christ as my Savior and Lord as a result of reading this book.

_____

NAME

_____

ADDRESS

_____

CITY   STATE/PROVINCE   ZIP/POSTAL CODE

_____

PHONE NO. (DAY)   E-MAIL ADDRESS

Please check the appropriate box(es), then clip this form and mail it to the following address. You can also email your information to: thevoice@vom-usa.org. If you live outside the U.S., see the websites listed on page 205.

The Voice of the Martyrs
1815 SE Bison Rd.
Bartlesville, OK 74006

For a list of affiliate offices, visit:
internationalchristianassociation.org.